The Taste

Sig

Uncovers the emotions in

MW00965085

"The Taste Signature" is a .... than produce a heavy tome built upon various constructions and different aspects of a single central new thought, here you will find a multitude of new ideas packed into 120 pages. The book is primarily for the food and drink marketing world.

Taste preference is driven by the emotions you associate with the flavours. This pairing of emotion and flavour is dependant upon the culture in which you grow up. Essentially through life you "learn" this preference. So while some flavours are inherently liked by mankind, most foods are a combination of tastes and thus are composed of a multitude of unconscious learnt messages.

If you understand the emotional messages triggered by the journey through the mouth of the taste and texture of the experience, the impact of the visual, aroma and aftertaste elements, it is possible to deconstruct the taste and understand the contribution to the delight created by each of the possibly 120 flavours contained within the taste. If the emotions are all positive ones, the consumption will be enjoyed. If the messages are, however, negative, the eat will be less delightful!

The scientific community has an incomplete understanding of taste, they know how it is detected but not the source of its delight or of peoples preference for one flavour over another. For 20 years Thornton Mustard has researched the basis of preference throughout the world working with the consumer in one and a half hour sessions, with over 22,000 people on 2214 product developments for the brands you see depicted on the cover. The Taste Signature describes and discusses a number of general hypotheses, which have been uncovered, constructed and found to be robust through that work.

Because our work has to be discreet we are restricted to general learnings but in four instances where the brands have won marketing awards and the information is therefore in the public domain, it is possible for us to be more specific."

I hope you enjoy the book.

Thornton Mustard

THE MARKETING CLINIC, BAYFIELD HOUSE, LYDFORD, DEVON,
EX20 4BH   TELEPHONE 01822 820 224   FAX 01822 820 447
e-mail thorntonmustard@themarketingclinic.freeserve.co.uk

The Taste Signature®

Uncovers the emotions behind the tastes of the world's leading brands

Thornton D Mustard

ISBN 0 9545014 0 3

Published by:
The Marketing Clinic
Bayfield House
Lydford
Okehampton
Devon
EX 20 4BH

Design & production co-ordinated by:
The Better Book Company Ltd
Warblington Lodge
Havant
Hampshire PO9 2XH

Printed in England

Contents

THE TASTE SIGNATURE

PART ONE

The Influence of Taste in Everyday Life

CHAPTER ONE

Delight in Flavour

Flavour lifts our spirits, it stirs us to delight. We are passionate about its preparation and presentation. Yet we are bereft of the ability to communicate more than headline responses.

Taste is a sense about which we comprehend little. Much of life is passed eating and drinking. More spent planning, evaluating and purchasing ingredients and idly reflecting on food. All of us discuss what we see and hear. We are elegantly articulate about colours, the sounds of our world and other human voices. We remain strangely tongue-tied, all but mute when describing taste. At least we know what we like. But do we?

While some foods we enjoy all our lives, with others we find our responses appear to evolve, seemingly as we get older. Many foods and especially drinks seem particularly enjoyable in certain circumstances, moments, seasons or geography. Yet at other times the same item is hardly pleasant at all, perhaps even downright unattractive. Out of place the flavour loses its bliss.

Like music, some tastes seem to be classics or standards. Others drift in and out of fashion and appropriateness. Indeed the taste experience is not unlike music, which also has a deconstructable arithmetic base, in that it is far more complex than it at first appears. For it is within that complexity that the reason for the imperceptible drift in popularity of certain eating and drinking experiences occurs.

When describing flavour most people manage an inadequate four or five stumbled words. Even the great literary figures do little better if at all. Yet we have very complex emotional reactions to food and drink that underscores and frequently determine that preference.

The consumption of a taste is a journey. It starts through the eyes, is investigated by the nose and evaluated and re-evaluated both in taste and texture through the different receptors of the mouth until it is swallowed. It vanishes, leaving behind both its aftertaste, significant emotion and in many instances a physiological reaction.

This convoluted journey, probably triggering well over a hundred conscious and unconscious thoughts and feelings, is a complex medley that contributes weightily to the quality of our lives. Yet all of this is truncated in social discourse to two or three words, mainly relating to simple preference.

Perhaps our poor skill springs from our evolution. The effectiveness of the individual senses to first detect danger causes flavour to be left far behind in the development race of the senses, losing out to sight, touch, hearing and olfactory or smelling skills. A food's taste does after all have be very heavily disguised indeed before we are unable to detect it as bad or worse, poisonous. Maybe the skill simply evolved as far as was necessary for our survival. Therefore its lower priority never drove the necessity of full language development.

Yet we retain vivid judgement. Instinctively we know light red fruit as a juice drink is a short summer season taste and tire of it easily. Pure strawberry drinks, unmixed with dairy fat, never catch on. Yet dark red, purple and black fruits are comforting, sustaining and do not exhaust our delight. Blackcurrant has a long history of success. Is it innate instinct or something else?

This wholly inadequate disconnect between the eating experience and our ability to communicate about its joy or otherwise, is now starting to become more of an issue. Today if we are affluent of country or self we can eat any foods or combination of foods, from around the world, almost any day we chose throughout the year. This has given us a diet and flavour stimulation that is of a completely different magnitude from that experienced by our surprisingly recent forefathers.

Today we greatly enjoy these wonderful new and complex food arias that we have, but we lack the ability to verbally express that joy to our friends and families. Our body language however is more informative. As the launch of new brands increasingly becomes prohibitively expensive, the marketer has to exploit his current brands and somehow utilise this over abundance of new tastes and textures to refresh and widen the appeal to his users. But often with older brands the loyal consumers are melting away. They seem less enamoured, less dependant on the brand. The product within the brand seems to fulfil and satisfy the consumer less. Why might this be?

Firstly today's consumer has met, experienced and enjoyed or otherwise a far wider range of actual flavours, twists on flavours or textures than the consumer of the day when that brand was created and first launched. Pivotally the emotional meaning of some of the taste characteristics within the brand no longer say to today's consumers what they once did in the brand's growth years. The individual taste and textures within the product and especially the way they combine may no longer be fashionable.

During the course of that convoluted journey from eye to stomach, will be some messages which are no longer appropriate. Within the flavour melody created some notes will now jar, be out of tune or be triggering emotions which are now unacceptable. Today a heavy sour rear mouth taste in a lager suggests an aggressive inebriation, and so the social teenager tends to avoid such a brand. A few great brand names died for this very reason

If we deconstruct the whole taste journey of a food or drink, we will find well over two hundred individual tastes, visual or aroma notes, plus nearly as many emotional responses that they trigger. Is it likely that all of those have the same meaning to a consumer today as they did a generation ago? Hardly. In truth, the very fact that these tastes are seen as the property or a previous generation frequently causes their demise.

Consider the visual, literary and performing arts, of a generation ago.

Here, clearly, appreciation has changed. Moved on. It should not surprise our marketer to find that his brands consumption experience is enjoyed in a different fashion to that in which it was perhaps only ten years ago.

He or she carries out quantitative research studies of new taste variations, in a sweeping search for improvement and either finds no perceivable difference in the scores returned, or a difference in preference which she cannot diagnose. In the first instance, he changed the wrong things, in the second she may have changed the right things but in the wrong way. It's not easy. The speed of plot development of old films provides a parallel to such change. Yesterday excitement is now slow, mundane, ordinary. Many racy and thrilling movies, gripping in their day anaesthetise current audiences.

If a Need State is a set of practical and emotional requirements of a specific eating occasion, most are very subject to change. Not only can the internal requirements of the state evolve or change. But as society alters, the very Need States' importance and frequency of occurrence will also alter. It will mutate, It may disappear. New Instances emerge. The old foods become stateless of need. Who eats bubble and squeak nowadays?

This conundrum is further complicated by the almost certain fact that his product is not being eaten in the same Need States. Life has changed so enormously from formal meal locations and prohibitions over eating between meals to a circumstance of individual meals, grazing and a massive preoccupation with balance of diet. The eating Need States have been revolutionised. Together with this the ingredients we consume have developed with astonishing acceleration.

What is truly extraordinary is that any company should imagine that their product is just as appropriate as it always was. With such life changes, is it likely? They have changed their advertising, their packaging, even perhaps their brand name or at least its graphics, even the point of distribution and relative pricing. Others change pack sizes, product bite sizes, and migrated to chiller or freezer.

Distribution and competitive set continuously swerve and shuffle. If marketers deconstructed the full taste experience and understood all of the messages and their relevance, positive, negative or even neutral, delivered by the consumption of their product, this would unlock far more fundamental reasons for its growth or decline. It would be helpful if their users truly enjoy the consumption of the product. Take Kit-Kat. The "melt", of which more later, of its wafer is fast, clean and both accentuates the chocolate taste but also cleans it from the mouth. You enjoy the chocolate but it's light. It reinforces the crisp snap of the first bite. Together they represent the Taste Signature, simply and with clarity. All are modern food taste messages so the brand prospers.

Cereals suffer. Their core Need State, breakfast is vanishing. They need milk, an unfashionable taste, sticky and cloying. Frequently eaten without sugar, so the mouth is left less stimulated. So both Need State and taste experience is anachronistic The mental refreshment of crunchy foods is a popular contemporary emotion. Cereals could have become snacks, but missed the opportunity.

The pattern of preference in your market and amongst your competitive set is moving, it is dynamic, changing and in constant flux.

Just because your consumer is unable to express this to you because of their void of taste descriptions does not mean that all is well.

On the numerous occasions we have resolved these problems for the very big brands in what the Mars European and Innovation Director once described as the "Bluest of blue" client lists, we found that only a very few notes within a drink or food contribute negative messages. But you do have to find which they are. Toning these down enables other tastes within the product to emerge more strongly. This re-orchestration supported by the rest of the marketing mix can re-energise the brand to give it a much improved future.

You have to adjust to meet both new or changing Need States plus consumers whose values and associates tastes that reinforce these values are in constant flux.

This book examines the various and inter-related aspects of flavour and the psychological meanings they engender with the public. Only those case studies that have been published, normally by the client to win marketing awards, are discussed in any detail. Also it's reasonable to talk about the products of clients competitors. The commercially sensitive detail of work must remain, as the Greeks would say appropriately in this context "behind the teeth".

Because, by its very nature, the work consisted of a series of research and development projects for the clients shown on the cover, the construction of this body of knowledge has not been built upon strict scientific principals. However, during the period of time, 4,674 consumer groups of an average of an hour and a half's duration were run, with a total of over 22,000 people, concentrating exclusively upon their opinions of over 2,412 products or development formats, whether they be food or drink. This provides the opportunity for the discovery and evolution of numerous insights into the subject. Indeed no other company anywhere even remotely approaches this level of specialised experience.

In nearly every case, the work was broken into two major stages, the first of which was to understand the situation and set up hypotheses for improvements. The second level of the work was to evaluate those improvements prior to the client making formulation, recipe or positioning changes for their brand. Inevitably therefore the establishment of specific hypotheses in each of the instances was core to the project. But over time it became clear that generally applicable rules about the ways in which tastes work or otherwise emerged.

The specific learnings about brands are of course the property of the individual client for which they were discovered, and none of those details are published here.

During the twenty years that this body of work represents, it has been possible to create general theories about how the consumer responds to the stimuli of flavour taste and mouthfeel. Subsequent researched experience has shown these hypothesise to be robust. It is these general learning's that provide the building blocks for this book. Enjoy it.

The "Taste Signature" of a brand uncovers the emotions of consumption and the taste details that drive those emotions. Often serious clients ask us to add the visual, colour, shape, texture, movement and tones that signal the flavours. These greatly enhance the completeness of the positioning and help with advertising execution.

CHAPTER TWO

Aroma Stirs Our Emotions

Everyone has a favourite location. An activity or moment at that place that is particularly valued. It may be a pastime, a hobby, a sport, a vacation, a process of travelling, a view, or just being there. It may well be shared with another. But in it they perceive a particular delight. It might stimulate anticipation, excitement, simple ease or a much more complex basket of emotions. What is inescapable is the pleasure that is derived in their emotional response to that specific circumstance. It might be relaxing, peaceful, dangerous even. But they like it.

It is within the emotions that the reward delivers.

These moments are made up of a multiplicity of stimuli that collectively cue these valuable responses. A selection of senses are variously involved in capturing the information that produces this mosaic of responses. If everything is just right then the reward is felt. Small variations in the stimuli can break that mosaic and the magic is gone. Interestingly if sufficient of the key stimuli connect, the mind 'recognises' the pattern, the experience "Signature" and the familiar feeling kicks in, although the context can be quite different. Of course the unfamiliar is also gathered in through the senses.

Of these, sight is the dominant vehicle for information. We hold our valuable experiences in mental imaging form whenever we can. No surprise then that we all collect so many photos. Sound is powerfully appreciated as well. We are reasonably adept at recalling the audio elements in these magical moments that we value. Touch is important also – this provides great detailed information – the weight, the warm, the smoothness, the abrasion, or the luxuriousness. That which we touch and we like, we easily recall. Perhaps never forget.

Taste will contribute pleasure and stimulation where relevant. Aroma will tend to be more elusive, less obviously connected and frequently not consciously noticed during the experience.

No one will question the ability of sound and particularly music to stir emotions. It does it in predictable and repeatable patterns.

We can choose our mood by selecting our music. This makes the audio impact extremely important in the contribution it makes to people's feelings. It is arguable if sound isn't more effective in driving feelings than sight.

Teens who experience wider mood swings than most other age groups often ground and control their state of mind by music, but also by repeat watching of specific videos. Computer games create the same effect of delivering a familiar and predictable mood. Useful at an age where the individual is under threat from treacherous hormone torrents.

But here we're interested in the insidious, subtle, insistent and persistent emotional messages that come from aroma. And it appears to be derived in a slightly different fashion. Very often it's direct to the unconscious.

Smells are particularly relevant to our own individual and personal experiences. We have very poor vocabulary for their description. Perhaps we never needed that language for survival. But they intrude just when we are least expecting it. They trigger powerful and difficult to deny emotional and psychological reactions.

If our valuable moment is the relaxation in good company and the environment in which we enjoy that, then the aromas of hearth, home and pub will be strongly associated with those benefits. If on the other hand it's the warm sweet notes of holidays and the tropics, then those aromas will be paired in our mind with the feelings of those occasions.

The fresh acrid smell of sports crowd excitement, the distinct sweetness of mown grass and soft mellow country smells of cricket, or the exhaust fumes and hot oil aroma of motor sports. The cooking and alcohol notes of fine food, or the special smells of intimacy. All of these become paired with emotive responses. We learn these connections. They frame many a life.

As you run through the above examples, your reaction is very individual, some of these circumstances mean a lot to you, others frankly nothing. Some may even be negative. Does this mean we're smelling different odour characters in the aroma? Unlikely.

Or is it perhaps that the value of these experiences accords individual meanings for different people. This is what makes smell so fascinating. Each person will attribute different values to different

THE TASTE SIGNATURE

aromas depending on their own experiences of their encounters with those smells.

If your best holidays have been in Spain, the construction of the aromas that you value would be radically different from some one else who experienced delight in the hot and sweet Middle East or with the rich warm dusky musky aroma of Africa. If horse racing was particularly enjoyable to you, then the clean hay and fresh sweat smell of horses would always bring you joy. Or maybe recall your losses.

The crisp dryness and fresh ink smell of a new book could mean eager anticipation to one individual. The smell of grease paint and stale furniture mean theatre and eager anticipation to another enthusiast. So the value and response we give to different aromas depends very strongly on our own individual experience, and that which stirs our soul. Once we have built our personal encyclopedia of aromas and emotions, paired together, usually in our salad days, we have them for life.

Once learnt, smells work in the inverse fashion. The smell of fresh crisp clothes and sophisticated fragrance might transport one shopper to incredible highs, but the smell of coffee might cause another to anticipate yet another challenging day. For another the coffee aroma cues social fun. Aromas trigger memory and the associated emotions, as long as the bouquet of smells finds a sufficiently good match for recognition in the archives of the mind.

Smells therefore cause us to react but the reaction is dominatingly an emotional one. The connections are not with heavy practicality but with the feelings that have become paired and associated with those particular aromas. These will vary for each individual and be markedly different for the two sexes and previous generations. But is it all acquired personal learning? Are all smells this personal?

Clearly not, some are heavily learnt and we don't all share the same responses. But others appear instinctive, with all people reacting in a similar fashion. The smell of burning might create different levels of concern, but we are all aware when it's not cooking and when it's dangerous. It's interesting to observe how individuals react to the smell of African predators. The heavy musky stale meaty notes make us all uneasy, unsure and very keen to find out the source of those particular aromas. Of course a fireman might diagnose the smouldering aroma as emanating from particular constructs of building materials, and the lion tamer might even picture an individual lion of which he were particularly fond, when the big cat smell permeates their nostrils. But their olfactory sense has been trained to evaluate, to judge and distinguish.

We can all smell running water, even though it's at the edge of our consciousness and all adults react to the aroma, attractive or otherwise, of the opposite sex. Is it aroma that enables even very small infant boys to recognise, even without visual clues, other boys and sets off the competitive cooperative male bonding?

So aroma spectacularly triggers emotional responses. You are walking along and suddenly, almost before you are aware of the smell itself, you are feeling the emotional response. Whether it's uplifting, causes anxiety or inquisitiveness. The response is very fast, very individual, except for those generic smells to which we all respond in a similar way. It is extremely powerful and motivating when a personal nostalgic experience is engaged. We all know the reek of money. The warm neutral cleanliness overlaid by expensive cloth, woods, leather and deep padding, and even perhaps just that hint of the folding luca itself.

One of the more interesting of emotions seems to be one of achieving civilisation. A human being spends an enormous amount of time eliminating, covering up the dominating natural smells. We're as ill at ease with those as we are with the obvious aromas of dirt, disease and disfunction. There is almost a ladder of aromas that signal and reinforce progress up the hierarchy of needs. We seem to need the edge of consciousness reinforcement that the evidence about our society's progress up life's ladder is confirmed by each of our senses.

Interestingly, aroma appears to create a wider and more complex range of emotions than we have language to describe. We know how to feel, often what to do, but can't describe the smell other than to name the source, Lion. It is almost as if the mammalian or even the reptilian brain that picks up and classifies the smells is happier with instructive responses – do I fight, do I flee? Is it a potential mate? Is it food? Is it a good drink?

So if aroma triggers these primordial reactions, how does its close relative's taste and flavour fit in? How is it these are liked, loved or perceived as indifferent? Scientists will say there is no flavour, it is all smell. Maybe this is too simple. Most flavours have a taste element of sweet, bitter, sour or salty within them, many have more than one. The true flavour message is a combination of aroma and taste, working synergistically to provide a stimulus.

Tastes are different because these are served to us in a controlled and sequential fashion. We meet very few for the first time without a written and courteous introduction. A small child starts their taste experience with milk of course, and for the rest of their life the vanillic notes present in mothers milk will serve to relax, calm and make them feel safe and secure.

After this other tastes are introduced. These arrive with labels attached. The child cannot read, but it can most assuredly sense its parents mood and anticipation. The food offered with a smile, indeed with an eagerness, from those around the baby suggest that here's a taste that's going to be great. But first of course, the baby has nothing against which to relate this. After all they only know the taste of milk, and therefore they will ape the reactions of their parents and tend to enjoy those early flavours, if the parents suggest they are exquisite. But there is a complication…

At first the baby is given very diluted taste experiences with very little sweetness or salt. Both of which are such strong notes, too powerful for the baby taste reception. The child is unable to enjoy it and will reject it out of hand. But as time goes by, so the balance of that which is offered, selected entirely by the parents and the society in which the child is bought up, begins to form a pattern. The balance between sweet tastes, good tastes, light tastes, savoury tastes, all is fed to the child together with a recommended emotional response, that the parents learnt earlier in life themselves. And the child follows this.

The mother is smiling, eyes dancing with anticipation, the baby thinks great, this is going to be good, and thus ice cream arrives. If there are stern faces suggesting this will do you good, then you are likely to meet your first… brussel sprout.

Children are extraordinarily sensitive to parental mood and so the belief structure, more of their mothers than the fathers, about diet will be served up with each introduction to the child.

If your mother believes in a fruit/vegetable orientated sweet spectrum, that's what you'll meet and interestingly, that's what you'll tend to enjoy for life. If savouriness or mild spiciness is the societies view, then again these tastes you learn to like, value and enjoy.

So why do children apparently experiencing the same food and taste introduction evolve different palate choices? The order sequence amongst you and your siblings has a considerable impact on how you approach life. In general terms, first children are expected and trained to be successful in life, and last children indulged with middle order children needing to fight for their identity and special treatment. So if the total parental attitude towards a child depends on its position within the family, the chances are that they won't be meeting food with the same introductions.

Often the elder children will have an equal to the parents, and perhaps superior, influence over their younger brothers and sisters. They are liable to bend, twist, modify and add to the delight of or overly criticise in their demeanour the food that is being introduced. Most children rapidly learn that their elder siblings are more in tune with their own views on nearly everything that are their parents. The desire to join in and copy brothers and sisters is hot wired and constructive. It is nearly impossible to create a proper test for this acquisition of preference. So we are back to the predictable debate of nature or nurture.

However, the fact that different parts of the country produce different flavour preferences strongly suggests that it's much more nurture than nature. You learn to like what those around you also enjoy.

A Scot has the sweetest tooth in the UK, and in the North East there is high tolerance and enjoyment of bitterness, and unsurprisingly, food availability greatly affects regional preferences. Those areas where pigs have been traditional reared, largely the middle strip across the country have a different view of pork than the Welsh who might have enjoyed lamb. Indeed in areas of traditional low mobility local and therefore cheaper food variations teach people a different palate.

So is taste entirely leant, or are there some tastes which are nature orientated, that everybody innately likes? The situation is exactly synonymous with that of the aromas. Though fire may always be dangerous, in general terms the human race likes chocolate, citrus fruits, sweetness and its burnt or cooked derivatives. Most cooked meat, the carbohydrates and more flavourful fruits are popular, as is dairy produce. But collection and process provides quite wide differentiation.

So, are all tastes leant on the mothers knee? Well no, they are not. But the circumstance of the encounter with a new taste or flavour, whether it is a pure or natural taste or combination blend or cooked recipe of flavours, is very much determined by the environmental situation in which it is met. Its point of discovery. Its Encounter.

The teenager in all cultures wishes to experience the world in their own way within the safety of their own peer groups. As children move into teenage years, so their tastes are dominated by the discovery and the views of their friends at that point. The need to conform guarantees a herd response. That is the story of our third chapter.

CHAPTER THREE

Learning to Like Tastes

If taste preference really is acquired with only a few tastes innate, how then is it learnt in childhood? Why are so few tastes and even fewer great brands successful in a major way throughout the life span? Why do we find the preferred tastes of childhood, even if they are a complex mix, not surviving through the "Teenage Transition" into adulthood.

A child's physiology in flavour evaluation terms is quite different from that of the adult. The child's mouth contains significantly greater quantities of taste buds, which are covering the entire surface of the tongue and also the roof of the mouth and indeed there is some information being collected on the insides of the cheeks. At babyhood, these are not differentiated, they all collect the same message and feed it through to the brain. Therefore the baby and the small child will taste anything they are given with the volume turned right up.

The impact of the flavour will be far greater to a child than we will ever experience as adults.

It is no surprise therefore that tastes that babies can tolerate have to be very bland indeed. If you doubt this indulge in some early mixed feeds for infants and delight in the absolute void of taste and satisfaction.

There is no proven explanation for this but the most likely hypothesis is that babies digestive systems are incapable of handling food very far distant from milk and that these taste buds produce a reaction which says don't eat and therefore protects the digestion and therefore the child's health. It would also be very effective in stopping the child enjoying anything inappropriate it popped into a mouth that was much more taste and texture sensitive. Babies do put some extraordinary things in their mouths, dangerous and sharp objects being a speciality. Low flavour items like earthworms and insects provide taste variety. But babies tend not to poison themselves.

The baby therefore learns step by step each new taste always presented in a mild, easy, simplistic form. The movement over to solids is very gradual and meal ideas consist of a paste texture product with mixed elements from the future adult diet. Other single tastes fruits and starches such as in Europe bread again start out with the simplest most bland format, ie white bread.

Fats are also provided and unsurprisingly these are dairy based and relatively close to milk itself, butter being a perfect early food.

Of course these first foods and particularly the subsequent learnt diet are very culture specific. Once the child is weaned through the first simple foods and starts to eat those foods that reflect adult consumption, unsurprisingly we find huge cultural differences. Imagine a Mexican diet for an eighteen month old child and compare that with his Scandinavian equivalent. It would clearly be very markedly different. Even at that stage there would be the beginnings of contrast between the two palates and their training.

As the child begins to grow, so the foods are presented within an emotional context. This is a super taste and good fun; this is a treat; this is something you really need to eat to grow; this is good for you and so forth. The child is already being trained in both its palate and the meanings of some of the different flavours. By meaning this refers to emotional context. Training is taking place of the appropriate response, for that culture.

As the child moves to four and five, you find that its social context becomes more and more important and special child parties begin to occur with very considerable frequency, which accelerate further once they are at school.

These are of course with birthdays and Christmas the first celebrations. And in order for a celebration to be successful, the vast majority of people present must enjoy the food and drink. Therefore within each culture there's a measure of conformity. And that's developed into another phase of food and that is party food. Indeed in almost every culture, there are food items and drinks that are only eaten at parties. As the whole principle of a party is to provide a break from normality, and create a different emotional context which is fun and celebratory, so indeed those particular flavours become associated with those characteristics. It's easy to imagine the adult equivalent. Champagne.

In early life children tend not to like mixtures in contrasting tastes. Many eat the ingredients of a meal category by category. This is good practice because it reinforces familiarity and reduces the challenge and power of the taste message. The other technique is to mix everything together into one mass. Here the tastes neutralise each other, individual notes are less so the taste volume is down. Also any new potentially worrying tastes are buried.

Children use their superb observational and copying skills to evaluate foods and drinks just as much as any other area of behaviour. They soon become aware that their food is actually different from the food of their parents.

The more adventurous might ask to try parental food, the rest are happy to stay within their own current taste palate. If we look at some of the characteristics of that earlier food, we find it a blander alternative to adult food, but it is also soft, easy to eat, requires less eating skills and tends to contain a less diverse range of flavours.

It is also stunningly repetitive. There are some children enjoying basically a limited range of six or seven items in various permutations for two or three years. Many males of the species continue this well into adulthood. Ask some restaurant chains about this and the lack of male food adventure. They will confirm this, with exasperation.

Let's look at three major food items and see how they remain in simplistic format. Children are more comfortable with the softness, ease within the mouth and delicacy and low flavour of white bread. Brown bread or whole grain bread is texturally difficult and texture is one of the areas where they remain most unadventurous.

A child can find 'bits' or lumps in anything. Some are convinced there are stones in the centre of strawberries! Minor textural differences assume the stone in the shoe syndrome. Ice-cream is a great food for children, but it's cold. Yoghurt does very well indeed, texture is soft and smooth taste subtle, but just a little too intrusive through its acidity.

Ice-cream flavours are unadventurous when they mirror tastes learnt elsewhere and the intrusion of secondary textures is very unpopular. Ice coldness reduces flavour impact, the texture creamy and easy dominates. Rice is in its simple uncomplex form is used for babies and the additives of more complex sophisticated rice formats are not used at that early life stage.

That worldwide favourite, chocolate, is again informative. So strong is the chocolate flavour that children cannot handle large, even in their terms portions, and require either that it is in mini portions, very small indeed, or that it is used and thus buffered with other ingredients.

So a filled confectionary bar with an easy interior and a relatively small amount of chocolate is diluted within the mouth. This makes it easier to handle.

Or it might be presented within a milk mix, with the chocolate level again low, present but not too powerful. Finally it might be a spread. You can observe products such as Nutella spread dominating some markets and chocolate coated biscuits others. Both are perfect ways to dilute chocolate. Textures remain soft, possibly as this age the child retains a sucking reflex still in residual form, while a true munch is yet to be developed. Softer uniform foods continue on as an important role for a long time.

The value of these soft gentle fatty creamy easy vanillic and marginally sweet taste characteristics are all associated with mother and being taken care of, feeling safe and secure within the home. It is no surprise that the baby is learning flavours' emotional messages. When later, even as the most sophisticated adult, he or she will still receive and gain comfort, relaxation and peace from these very characteristics whenever they eat them for the rest of their lives.

As he moves into adolescence the child continues to select, whether from kitchen cupboard fridge or indeed purchase with pocket money their choice. She remains surprisingly unadventurous, keeping to an extraordinarily low number of items, many of which continue to have this childlike suckability within them. Extreme foods in textural terms never get anywhere. Children adore crunchy foods, like crisps easily enough but granular or gritty food take some getting use to. The fast dissolve of sugar sweets provide texture in a friendly fashion. This taste palette remains stable until the teenage transition.

At first sight this appears to be triggered by puberty and indeed is heavily accelerated by that but it is usually commenced by the change to secondary schools, when the child moves to the school that will take them through the choppy seas of their teens to the shore of adulthood. This is an environment driven by the peer group structure, experimentation and searching for individual personality and the meanings of life. Not much to keep a person occupied!

As they have to experiment, so new ideas and experiences become seductive. Also they need to, always with regret, leave behind their favourite food brands from childhood. But if they experience troubles within their teen group, what is the first thing they will reach for? The old favourite foods from childhood, toys too.

But already many individual tastes will have been classified and restricted in their lifetime usage. A delightful example is children's medicines. In the UK, these tend to be packaged with strawberry flavour as this is an easy gentle taste that with much added sweetness masks effectively, but in the States, blackcurrant is used, which in fact is a heavier richer more rear mouth flavour but has the same effect. The UK uses heavy sugar to lengthen and de-seasonalise the mid mouth strawberry flavour in order to cover the medicinal aftertaste.

If you then move forward to adult life you find that you can't sell clear unsweetened or fat free strawberry tastes that easily in the UK and that blackcurrant, even on its own, is a wonderful indulgence flavour. The reverse generally applies in the USA where the strawberry taste tends to be blended with that of other berries to break the connection. But strawberry can be used in creamy rich texture with dairy ingredients which moves the point of impact of the taste within the mouth and this severs the learnt memory. The US uses cherry as a rich heavy fruity sweetness, in the role that blackcurrant performs in the UK.

By the time of the "Teenage Transition", the taste buds within the mouth are now organised into their adult format. Gone are the taste buds on the roof of the mouth and from within the cheeks and the taste buds on the tongue have become specialised. For instance those at the very tip of the tongue have become expert at detecting sweetness. Sourness is picked up along the sides of the tongue. Acidity within the pit of the tongue and bitterness at the very back of the tongue and a little in the throat.

What this means is that the only places within the mouth that the adults can actually taste those tastes, and the flavours carried with them are now fixed. This is at the basis of the whole process of how taste works in adult life. Flavours can be manipulated by their carrier so that the taste is extended in terms of its area of impact, but it is still gripped and largely restricted to these areas of detection.

The 'teenager', be it ten, eleven or twelve, has now left the haven of early school and is in an environment which is questioning of parental values. Culture and society powerfully influence the age of onset of this sensitivity.

In those cultures where family is put at the very top of the priority list, well ahead of the me society, the children tend to be more highly valued and more involved in adult interaction and events. This makes the questioning more gentle, occurs only when they are older and is more related to their own discovery of new, to them, experiences or food product forms.

In those cultures where the adults put themselves first, the children are inevitably of less importance. There, unsurprisingly, the rebellion occurs harder, faster and is more extreme. Remove the good role model and drive the hurricane of revolution.

But in any event this self discovery is now underway. As we all know this age works in groups discovering things collectively. Experiencing new things with your friends is a lot less stressful and dangerous and therefore you can be more adventurous than if you do it on your own. And in consequence teenagers worldwide wisely operate within these groups.

Fashion waxes and wanes, sometimes these groups are divided by sex, other times they are a collective and their group size also appears to vary. This may perhaps depend more on the size and need of the rebellion creating larger groups in order to produce conformity within the change. 'All of us think this so it must be true, and there are lots of us!'

In terms of food and drink, the first thing our sophomore teenager does is to reject and put behind them those items from childhood. So favourite foods like some chocolate biscuits or blackcurrant drinks which signal things of safety and security, now seem inappropriate. They scream lack of adventure, no newness or discovery. And they are of course the absolute antithesis of the latter. So risk becomes doubly attractive. Anything new thus becomes amazing! Things well known and of the parental generation are boring.

But arrayed in front of teenager are all the foods, drinks available to the adult. Their only inhibitors are flavour and money.

Let's use a UK example, but it has resonance in the structure of its learning process in other countries. This is alcohol. When first consumed, unless it is watered wine in Latin countries, alcohol arrives to be tested by a palate which has been oducated to enjoy soft, easy, sweet, creamy and savoury foods, and in drink terms, sweet, very sweet carbonated soft drinks. Fruit juice is a constant is its wide international usage but varies to an extraordinary and very unexpected degree, try Spanish orange fruit juice! UK also 'enjoys' the special squash drink, colourful, sweet and sweetened, refreshing but of doubtful taste heritage.

Alcohol, even in its mildest form is sour, bitter, challenging and to the initiate, absolutely disgusting. Separate generations have handled this in different ways, depending upon what's available. Currently alcopops make the transition easiest, whereas twenty years ago, beer mixed with lemonade to produce shandy worked on the same principle.

However, for our construct here the most important thing is that to the teen this unsavoury lager drink, which no one within the groups will admit to the other is unpalatable and all pretend to be enjoying as part of their group responsibility, of course creates inebriation.

This makes our early teens even more loquacious, bonds their group more closely together and they have a great time. Until they are sick. The English drink of cider is a UK initiator product and it's drunk often from large bottles, by a group in the park, behind the bike sheds, well away from adults eyes. They all become sick and because they are vomiting, the acidity and astringency already in cider become more so and this together with the simple apple fruitiness becomes fixed, taste and learned experience paired together within the memory.

Interestingly, ten years later, that child now an urbane smooth early twenties adult tries cider on a hot day and feels "childish". They don't know why this taste makes them feel silly, but it does. They drink only one glass. Even though it is very refreshing they switch to something else, confused and mildly embarrassed at how they feel.

What they do not realise of course is that their learnt experience of those two characteristics of simple fruitiness and strong astringency is triggering the emotional childlike reaction of that learned experience and causing them to reject the product.

All the cider industry had to do was to change the acidity which created the astringency so that it was still refreshing, but not as violently so, and alter the simple apple flavour into a sweet white wine note. This note was very fashionable and adult, and behold, the young teen was able to drink this product until oblivion. This was white cider.

It was heavily drunk for three or four years in the UK. At one point it was actually out-selling lager and beer amongst the start-up drinkers age groups. Amazingly it was not even recognised as a cider but as simply by a number of brand names. Why care about the provenance or classification of previous generations, recognise it by its name, its bar-call, its effect. It was of reasonable taste, very strong in alcohol and produced a lighthearted uninhibited drunkenness, largely without the aggression some premium lager of the day created.

Here is, in this cider case study, the powerful connection between taste and learned emotion, especially when they come in a combination, say of flavour and mouthfeel, as the original ciders did, act synergistically and produce a very definitive and clear, memorable and embarrassing response.

Depending upon the degree of rebellion our teenager will chose substances, foods and drinks, which the parents reject. Or choose food and drinks which are perceived as belonging to them, and their group, and not either to the previous generation or to their own childhood. Positioning and advertising to this teen group demands specific skills and experience. Coca-Cola are experts!

In general food terms, the teenager is pretty pragmatic. They eat for fuel, which they need in substantial quantities and simple but distinct taste foods are particularly enjoyed. Cheese, not a food much enjoyed by children except in its mildest creamiest format, now begins to be used. Other strong flavours such as sauces can be used with abandon, but with a little more sophistication than in childhood. Milk and cereals are particularly popular since these produce fast eating, lots of snack like texture, and interestingly still carrying the comfort message that is so important, especially when you are being adventurous. A teen with friends, a sometime child at home.

To return to our staples of bread, rice and chocolate; how have these evolved acting as prototypes for the rest of food. Breads become brown and crusty, thicker, chewier and toast is a huge enthusiasm. Crunchy, soft, cooked, noisey to eat and a carrier for anything! Rice is now received in dishes of spices, meats and ethnic dishes. Brown rice increases in popularity as do other rice types.

Chocolate can now be tolerated, starts being enjoyed in its various forms with incredible enthusiasm. It delivers energy brilliantly. When on its own it is an excellent comforting relaxing food with tremendous feelings of safety. When eaten with biscuits, it mixes in the security with the crunch and adventure to be attractive approachable, initially exciting then calming and safe. It reflects very well their life. Filled lines of chocolate are much used to give greater satisfaction, bulk, bite and chew. It provides instantly the energy teen life requires. Mild parental discipline over excessive chocolate eating helps guarantee its popularity.

We can see how it is extremely difficult for a food often expressed as a brand to succeed for the whole of a persons life. Few products can meet the needs of childhood together with the first requirements of teenage life. It has to metamorphosise into another format, be presented as a different brand and be experienced in a new fashion. It is those very encounters which we will examine next. How important is the moment of discovery and how this can so easily fix within the mind the role of those foods and brands.

Once in their twenties, individuals develop their own personal values. Relationships become serious, as does the whole of life.

Just as our teen left childhood products behind, so too does the true adult reject the behaviour of teenage years.

Groups become pairs. There is a search for a home where ones beliefs about oneself can be expressed in the design and décor.

Now the very foods and drinks of teenage years come under fire. It's time to move on. To enjoy more complex lagers, drier wines, adult foods and recipes. Tastes that signal the behaviours and beliefs of teenage years become an embarrassment. The consumer forges on with barely a backward glance.

It's hard for a brand to stay close to its users on such a series of migrations, obsessive, driven and desperate like the Wildebeest of East Africa. Clothes, movies, magazines, make-up for the girls and hairstyles for everyone – all deserted. What chance is there for foods and soft drinks that were identified with teenage lives attracting the necessary visas? Little or none.

CHAPTER FOUR

Understanding Discovery

It seems obsessive but people have a driven need to classify and organise their information. In order to do that when faced by a new experience they will immediately relate it to other events that they understand. They align this new experience as similar to something familiar yet different. This has the effect of creating a series of boxed ideas, all with their own mental labels. Into the appropriate one of which each new experience is hastily placed. Sometimes brusquely shoved.

Without question, this storing of data into pigeon holes helps the individual control the learning process. Thereafter the retrieval of ideas is as simple and swift as possible. This forces each experience to be described or encrypted into a very short descriptor indeed. Thus the new idea is held as a concept which is good, bad, modern, traditional, dangerous, safe, healthy, amusing or whatever.

This classification is very language dependant. For obvious reasons, the classification requires a name tag which at most seems to extend to possibly three or four words. We notice this single thought transference in brand descriptors, those short lines, often called tag lines, that go with a brand and are repeated endlessly. A personal favourite is the liberation army, which is always the one that "comes to enslave you". Indeed politicians use this message shorthand a great deal, and when they use it, it's a soundbyte, sadly usually a half truth. Sorry, a quarter truth.

The great advantage, or is it disadvantage, that this contributes is that it enables the individual, once they have classified this experience, person, concept, food or drink, not to have to think about it ever again. Whenever the idea pops into the mind, it arrives with its short list of word descriptors permanently attached. The person can feel comfortable and familiar with it. It requires no re-examination. Heineken refreshes the parts that others cannot reach.

Inevitably of course this means that each one of these pigeon holes is a distortion into which the idea, or product has been pushed and from which it will find it very difficult to escape. The thought is immutable at that moment. This labelling, or even "branding", of the idea tends to become fixed unless there are major reasons for a rethink or re-evaluation. Humans are lazy, so this occurs only very infrequently.

That makes the eastablishment of this first understanding at the "Encounter" a critical event. This first meeting with a brand is likely to determine its entire future.

The problem arises when individuals, a group or a corporation needs to change the whole battery of thoughts or indeed the pigeon hole into which their brand has been placed. They need to coerce people to look at it again. See it with a fresh and open mind. This is not easy.

It's even harder when the new concept is so fresh and original that there is no current language existing to describe it. Later in Chapter Six we discuss "Wellness", a word created to describe a certain belief structure. Yet that word is cripplingly inadequate. It doesn't do the job and therefore the concept is vague, difficult and interpreted by different people in a number of ways.

In marketing of course there are numerous methods of encapsulating strategically the concept at the heart of a brand. Onions, targets, 'T' plans and many more forms of positioning structure exist.

Yet all of these are essentially similar and involve at the centre some core values, limited to one to three words, and around this periphery are various support values. These are maximised or manipulated in order to guide the manic creators of advertising, promotions or packaging so as to relay a planned disciplined strategy to the consumer.

These structures rightly encompass practical, logical, emotional and inspirational values together with those that reinforce and support peoples self image. The difficulty however is the sheer quantity of elements within the positioning. These will assuredly have trouble squeezing into and then being constrained by the size of the human mental pigeon hole. All cannot be digested. Many will spill out!

This brings us to the issue of an individuals first meeting with a new experience. In life, very few experiences, or in our case foods, and drinks are met without some form introduction. This contains the pigeon holed thoughts of those who wish to influence or indeed create that introduction.

New brands may be met anytime in life. But most new base flavours are contacted in childhood. So with every new food or drink a child encounters, everything comes with its own descriptor, voice over or health warning.

These may be directly expressed by the parent or be picked up through the attitude or the people around. Yet most telling of all are the circumstances that surround that first consumption. People learn very early that the mobile emotions within people mean that there is some lack of consistency in their parents attitudes.

When a child feels that is the case, then they take their cues from that which is more trustworthy. Inconsistent parents therefore confuse children. The children have to look elsewhere for the data against which they can evaluate the new experience.

Thus, a mother might have told a child on numerous occasions before that something is nice when their own experience says it isn't. She is giving it to me at breakfast and therefore one thing I can be sure of is that this is a breakfast food, not a treat. I will align it, compare it and contrast it with other breakfast foods. Likewise, on a cold or hot day when I'm being offered this outside meal times, I query is the weather relevant to the choice of this food. The introduction may come at a party, or at a moment of great seriousness. The child will learn to depend upon these cues just as much as any propaganda. Probably more so!

The "introducer" is critical as well. My big brother might always try and get me to try things that I'm not ready for. Whereas my uncle might be the exact opposite, and very conservative.

My friends vary. I classify them by what I might have learnt about them. I review their introductions through what I know about their beliefs behaviour and their motivation. This is why good brand names accelerate early consumer trial. The risk is reduced. You partly know them already. Early car manufacturers used animals to symbolise their cars personalities. No contemporary shorthand has bettered that concept.

The environment also makes a great deal of difference. Is it being introduced in an expensive place, in a fun relaxed fast food environment. Is the event abroad, is it in a small village or in the middle of the largest city? Are the people around relaxed or quite formal, are they serious or perhaps merry? Is the place exclusive? Finally, what have I heard about similar food/brand/drink in the past. So how can I anticipate it?

Notice the way that at the moment of the Encounter, many more questions are being asked than will be the next time. Indeed any time in the future. Once the product has been classified and pigeon holed, no more questions are necessary. Nor will they be voiced far less thought.

It's no surprise therefore that pigeon holing is essential, for without it one would have to relearn every situation from scratch. Much time would be lost to relearning what had already been understood. This means in real terms that the intellectual and emotional effort placed against any new experience is both substantial and comprehensive. It will not be repeated. Thus, once a new experience has been thus classified, re-classification will not readily occur.

Thus the "Encounter" is the experience that determines an inflexible opinion.

Newness is very attractive to the human being. If it's new we are on our guard, but equally fascinated. Our internal feelers bristle driven to classify.

This may be partly due to the way in which newness forces the individual to call up all their previous experiences in order to evaluate this fresh situation. This heightens the value of the new experience and the classification process becomes an adventure. It is particularly exciting an the individual knows the fun will never be as intense again.

Newness is of course also frightening for things are more likely to go wrong. The ideal for the individual is that there is a large, maybe eighty precent, content of familiarity which enables them to classify, and feel fairly secure but a small, say twenty percent element which is new. This makes it exciting, is sufficient to trigger this "new encounter analysis" which in itself is fascinating and motivating, a true emotional experience.

Indeed if the newness content is too great, such as learning to operate a computer for the first time, or constructing one of these delightful DIY products.

The individual can be enormously put off at even the thought of the challenge. They may not engage.

It's also immediately apparent that different ages behave differently and once the child has moved into the teenage acceleration, these new experiences become stunningly attractive. Pre-teens the sense of adventure may be less if the child's hand wasn't being held by friend or family.

Equally in their greying years people lose the willingness to experiment. They long for familiar patterns and events. They are drawn like insecure children to routine. Newness again becomes a threat.

Therefore unless newness is presented in the disguise of the familiar with a twist the current repeated patterns of behaviour usually described as "loyalty" persist. Your brand remains untried. The marketing executive must really manage that encounter!

The food or drink encounter of course obeys these rules but has some specific difficulties. The central one of these is language. Because we tend to think first in visual terms and by use of pigeon holed, pre-digested thoughts and can only think in the main with the words we know and the pictures we have stored, it makes the meeting of new tastes and smells quite difficult. We react but do not articulate. The learning decays with terrifying rapidity, unless fixed by an effective descriptor.

The emotional associations that go with smells are also used when dealing with tastes. But taste is less obviously emotive and is more complicated in its construction than aroma.

Taste can be broken down into the anticipation from the eyes, with some support from the aroma. But it is then subject to a taste journey through the mouth and the swallow. This will involve the impact of different flavours on different parts of the mouth and of course, classically the aftertaste. It also suffers from the major complication introduced by texture.

This mouthfeel contains as many interesting pre-learnt, often from childhood and suitably pigeon holed perceptions regarding individual flavours. This produces a complex tapestry of experiences.

We would expect to find in most foods or drinks well over one hundred elements of taste, texture and aftertaste. And each of these carries with it its own individual learnt meanings of logic and emotion. Obviously some dominant others recessive.

From childhood we learn taste by taste, texture by texture this complexity of meaning about each of those individual in mouth experiences.

Children with their multiplicity of taste receptors receive the maximum stimulus but the minimum understanding. If it's too complex, the newness element too high they cannot decode and process the food. It is also why children only enjoy simple unchallenging food. Otherwise the messages would be too terrifying.

The rule of eighty percent familiarity and twenty percent newness would then be broken and the child would have inadequate sources of reference and reject the food outright. Those with children will have enjoyed the theatre of this!

So this learning of tastes is a brick by brick, structure upon structure building up from childhood until it represents a city of experiences where few of the streets have names. Which makes following the taste map problematical.

Humans, at least in the West, do not discuss taste in any way at all. Spontaneous thoughts or discussion about a taste might product half a dozen words for a taste which has one hundred plus elements. We are simply not sufficiently interested to carry out this discourse. Of course the same applies to smells.

Undoubtedly, if dogs could talk, a huge portion of their vocabulary would be about smells. They would have a much more detailed construct of pigeon holes into which different taste characteristics were placed. This is akin to the famous Eskimo use of twenty seven words to describe snow. This is completely beyond the comprehension of anyone in countries where snow is an infrequent occurrence.

So how does the human pigeon hole these complex experiences in such a way that they can be handled? If they don't pigeon hole they can't make decisions, they can't make choices and everything becomes a completely new experience. It would have to be learned from scratch each time. Rather like the short memory goldfish.

They aren't going to classify the new food by descriptive details of taste with the emotions attached. That would use up too many pigeon holes for the size of the task in hand. It's not justified. What people actually do is break foods and drinks down by Need States.

Let's just chose one Need State in order to keep our eye on the concept without getting bogged down in the detail. Our need is to categorise the idea as simply as possible.

Let's look at "Stimulating Snack". In order to stimulate, a food needs to have a very clear and obvious first taste. This needs to be strong, easy and not too complicated. To carry that taste, either sweetness or saltiness or a combination needs to be present. The salt will stimulate the taste buds and accentuate the taste and the sweetness will help carry that flavour. Fat can be used, but in low quantities; if it is excessive, the texture will be inappropriate.

The texture needs to be nibbly, crunchy, involving the front teeth. Preferably this process should be noisy and intrusive so that all the senses including the auditory ones are also involved. This initial crunching and fast taste delivery awakens the mind.

By triggering the mind in this way, it stops it thinking about what it was preoccupied with immediately before the crunch. It provides an opportunity for a change of thought direction. Because of the pace with which this crunchy high taste small piece snack delivers, it will speed up the thinking process and therefore make the person feel more alert. They then become more awake. This awakening starts the break.

Self-evidently the items within the product need to be small, possibly eaten one at a time or a few crammed into the mouth together at once. Their taste needs to be all the same. If there is a variation in taste, then that will stop this generation of speed of thought and cause the person to stop, reflect and diagnose what all the different tastes are. That's too intrusive. Equally if the product was too difficult to select from its container and deliver into your mouth, that would again intrude and the stimulation would be lost. This is self evidently a very fast eat.

The product then needs to dissolve in the mouth pretty quickly; if it ends up being chewed as a heavy mass by the molars, then it is becoming too food like, too substantial.

In that instance the message the mind picks up is that here we have a real food item which is going to provide fuel and satisfaction and represents a real meal. At that point, if that were so, the consumer would start to re-classify the product and it would no longer give the signal 'snack' and the fun would start to evaporate. Now it would be fuel or sustenance, and serious.

Because it provides this change of mood, for most assuredly it does, is positive and upbeat in its character, it then is ascribed as fun, entertaining and enjoyable. It changes pace. Provides a break from the mundane. Gets rid of the responsibilities.

It is essentially a irresponsible break in the time continuum, and as such very enjoyable and welcome. It's fun. It fires the child within us to delight. We recall it fondly. When we eat it again the fun is re-triggered.

Also of course you probably will finish it before you are ready to. So the pack is gone almost before you are aware that you started to eat it. This again provides a break and accentuates the level of stimulation. Should you eat it for too long, then the taste would start becoming predictable. The stimulation would slow down. The taste buds would become tired. The effect would evaporate.

It's no surprise therefore that these products are contained in small bags, they are never individually wrapped, they are more savoury than they are sweet. They are high on taste. Because stimulation and newness is more attractive to younger people they tend to be eaten more by younger people than older ones. New dangerous, intrusive, just ideal for a teenager. Guess who eats them?

If you put too much complexity of taste into the product, it becomes more sophisticated and requires more thought. If you package it too carefully you move it to a more formal occasions. If you make it too perfect, you can deliver the crunchiness but now you are delivering a measure of evaluation and indulgence. You move the product yet again away from that original particular Need State. It now invades a new Need State.

Let us not imagine that all snacks are stimulating and we can see at once that the stimulating snack has to have certain ingredients. If they are not there or the product is too sophisticated or complex, it will move out of that Need State and become something else. Perhaps a Sophisticated Social Snack?

Also and more importantly, a product that can be eaten in another way simply by changing the pace, flavour or size of the pieces can enter more Need States.

The snack market for instance has, depending upon how you break the definitions, half a dozen or so major Need States and many of the smaller brands are stuck in the Need State in which the consumer first encountered them. They don't escape from this prison for their characteristics inhibit their wider use. They never grow into big brands. They are too specialised in their niche.

The product has to be capable of being eaten in a flexible fashion so that people can enter it from more then one of the Need States. Then they can use it in other states. This leads onto much more frequent and heavier eating and resultant growth in the brand and its development.

Pack sizes, flavour changes, visual differences, proper size differences and pack configurations all can move a product on into other occasions. It's no surprise that multi-packs of snacks take it from stimulation into real food substitute as long as the product can be eaten in that format. If it can't then it will not expand sales, or at least not in that Need State.

Understand the detail of the Need State you are targeting. Also be very aware of neighbourhood Need States and the suitability of your item in that next potential situation. Make certain that taste texture duration in mouth and taste impact are emotionally and psychologically right. If not, don't launch. Finally manage the point of the encounter. This is your only chance to determine the mental shorthand, or pigeon hole into which the consumer will place your brand. Make it obvious, familiar but exciting and get it right.

In the next chapter we will look at how specifically these skills and lack of abilities are bought to bear on evaluating a new product at its Encounter.

CHAPTER FIVE

Fashions in Flavour

We have seen how the consumer dredges previous experience to make simple comparisons between what they have enjoyed before, or indeed not enjoyed, and the new experience being presented to them. In terms of food and drinks, the consumer will use all the available information in the sequence in which it is made available. The pack may be seen first, advertising may follow. Where it is first seen on sale will establish certain limits to its eventual use. Friends may mention the product, someone may be seen eating it. Each level of data is simplifying the possibilities or in badly thought out cases, confusing the recipient.

The key questions will be who is it for? When is it to be consumed? Which is its central Need State? And would it fit into the repertoire of foods or drinks that I personally use, on those occasions for which I judge it to be correct? Sometimes of course a product will simply be the fifteenth or more variation on the same theme. Just be another manufacturers or own labels supply of a specific product format. Very much a "me too".

But as we have seen in order to talk about it in a positive way the consumer needs to see a high familiarity content with a smaller element but an attractive one that appeals and makes it different and interesting. Makes it new.

Advertising the opinions of others and clues from the packaging are the first messages. To a far greater extent than the marketers tend to imagine, consumers do introduce products to each other and women do this more than men.

Indeed considering for whom the product is suitable, is part of the classification process. The individual might already have decided it is right for a certain friend, perhaps not even of their own generation, as part of the classification process. Many consumers find it easier to think in terms of for whom the product is, and pigeon hole it in that way because that ascribes to it values associated with that individual. This shortcuts the evaluation process and enables them to relate better to the idea.

Although the advertising industry would feel that their efforts were pivotal, they are really only a single but very important element. Of very great importance is the situation where the product is encountered.

If this product is met in a stylish and adventurous eating place, on display at the filling station, met in a nightclub, or spotted amongst similar ideas in their local grocer, all of these speak considerable volumes.

Once again they can observe the other people who may be purchasing or showing an interest and this helps classification. But it also gives an idea of the way in which this brand may or may not support their self image or their inner value structure.

If it's a food they will go further. They won't look at ingredient lists, in spite of government and manufacturers insistence that they do, but they will look at pictures and colours and pick up recognition of different ingredients. Product shots help greatly. This makes it possible to give a rough idea as to whether this might be liked as an eat. Suggests it could be appropriate for a certain point of purchase and the Need States that fit with that point of purchase. A sophisticated wine shop will add quality to any wine on display. A mix and match confection in Woolworths says something different. A kiosk at a fair something else again.

Do the ingredients look healthy, wholesome, light-hearted, chunky or even heavily indulgent? The brand name might be useful for hints, but frequently not. But the colours on the packaging will be very informative indeed. People have direct learnt correlations between colours and taste. Greens are healthy and fresh creamy colours are rich, and as they get darker they are more indulgent, heavier more satisfying.

Whereas some colours are extremely difficult. Blue in general terms is a non-food colour. It can denote freshness and coolness, but as it gets deeper and therefore has more meaning, so it starts to suggest non-food and as it shades into purple this is a strong poison signal. Metallic colours are fascinating as these nowadays suggest a lightness, freshness, a sugar-free or 'lite' idea. But not to an older generation

The classification of Need States is very extensive. Is this to be eaten to refuel you? Or for high taste impact? Or is it to revitalise you, refresh you mentally or calm, relax or even excite you? Is the food fun? Is it serious? Is it main stream or very occasion specific? And for who's occasion?

The consumer will go through this process, much of it in the unconscious mind by recognising patterns in the product presentation. Two or three elements together, from perhaps advertising, packaging, name or descriptor will be used to provide an anticipation of all of the above. And in instances where the product comes close to the individuals self image, then the question is will I feel reinforced in my view of self by this product? Will others think it appropriate to the Me I'm portraying? Is it something which I simply can't pay any attention to? Does it shout all the wrong things?

The conscious mind is very little involved. It might pick on a couple of aspects and give a second or twos thought. But today's consumer is very marketing savvy and is just as likely to regard that effort with cynicism as it is to take it on board.

The other element of this mix is whether it all rings true. Are all the messages singing from the same song sheet, or are there obvious conflicts? This leads us to the question of fit. Does the product promise heavy rich indulgence, or place itself in a rave scene? Does it promise energy, but also signals a heavy fat content? It fits but do I want both those two elements? More important, does it fit me?

Do I "recognise it" and, not in detail but in its use occasion and how it might eat, and identify with the idea?

There has been, as we all know, an extraordinary change in peoples food and drink consumption in recent years. This has left dissonant generations with completely different food requirements and in many cases, ones that are diametrically opposed.

Younger people being into lighter, frequent high taste experience, older people into richer, greater indulgences. These are variations on the inevitable changing needs as people age. Today it's very difficult, as we saw in the third chapter, not merely to appeal successfully from childhood through, all the ages of man and indeed woman. Foods and drinks have a very substantial fashion content in their acceptability.

This is driven more by the change of Need States than it is by a brand naturally aging or reaching maturity. There is much discussion about brand cycles and the need to rejuvenate older brands. In reality, what happens is that the Need States under pinning a brand become less appropriate to the society of the time. But also the various tastes and textures become similarly inappropriate, in the meanings they signal.

Let's sight a few brief examples. If we look at the heavy, sweet, rich, indulgent foods, largely typified by both old fashioned puddings, (notice the ready to mind critique built into that very phrase) and such products as cakes, based on cream, fruit and also cheese cakes.

Even the sight of such a product can trigger in the consumers mind the rich heavy feeling as it melts within the mouth and the weight or arrival in the stomach. The subsequent potential feeling of repleteness. To someone who is looking for some relaxation, some deep comfort and escape, this is immediately attractive.

However if another simply wants a sweet, clean taste to end a meal, then this provides too much bulk and substantivity for its level of taste delivery. It will also be seen as fattening, simply because of the obviously visual clues, of richness and sweetness so overtly on offer.

Yet this is an emotional rejection, relating to the indulgent Need State which is denied by many as entirely inappropriate to a modern healthy life style. But yoghurt is perfectly permissible. Of course with care, the individual could consume less fat, sweetness and caloric content by eating a small amount of cheesecake that by enjoying the ordinary size of yoghurt container. In reality therefore what is being rejected is the actual in mouth taste and texture of the cake, not the true calories consumed.

Another area of weakness in terms of judgement by the consumer is the ability to know whether they have eaten enough.

Here the human is very easily confused. Items of high taste satiate through the sheer weight of messages of flavour that are received by the brain. It is as though the mind says I've had so much taste, I can't really take any more, so I must be full.

We see this with ethnic foods where a very high taste delivery leads to a very early feeling of repleteness and the termination of the meal. Hunger returns with a vengeance in an extraordinarily short period of time.

But it is not only the ethnic foods that do this, Marmite also produces this response and is very effectively indeed. Many consumers use that particular brand effectively as a dietary product, finding its heavy satiating taste delivery, which over runs the taste buds, signals 'I've eaten enough'. Yet the caloric content is really only present on the carrier piece of bread or toast that has been used.

For fashionability, look at the movement of flavours within the beer market. Here, twenty years ago, in order to join the teenage group, the individual had to drink bitter. This is an extremely difficult and complicated product. So as to enjoy the alcoholic effect and its emancipation and to maximise the groups enjoyment and bonding as they experiment with new experiences, it had to be drunk. But it took six months or more of drinking a product that the individual simply didn't like before they acquired the taste and it became enjoyable.

The reason for that acquisition was that the rewards mentioned above were so great, (they were all emotional ones) that they justified the persistence needed. Eventually that taste cued the emotional benefits that a drinking session provided and these emotions were so attractive that the drink, paired with those, itself became enjoyable. The taste had been acquired.

The moment that lager was launched, and was trialed by the teenager versus bitter, it was immediately easier consumption, far less challenging. It only took six weeks to learn to drink. No one in their right mind was going to drink a product that took six months to acquire when one that took six weeks was available.

The demise of the British brewing industry was absolutely inevitable from that moment.

And indeed, since then lagers have got lighter, fresher, cleaner, less sour, less bitter, easier to drink, less challenging and therefore inevitably took over from those more complex tastes, at least for young drinkers. This is the classic taste acquisition route. It is repeated in many areas, coffee without sugar is another classic. Impossible to start with but acquired and preferred.

But the male palate tolerates bitterness better than the female and needs an ever increasing taste stimulation to provide the emotional satisfaction that comes from the flavour.

Bitterness and sourness are detected at the rear and sides of the tongue. What mid and rear mouth flavour does is make the individual reflect, ruminate even. Its slows down the thought processes and allows relaxation to occur. This is further re-enhanced by a less frenetic thinking sequence. Mid mouth taste impact appears to slow the heart rate, which in turn feeds back to the relaxation. The alcohol helps.

As more experiences of life are met as the drinker becomes older, so the complexity of issues and the reduction of the obvious black and whiteness of so many situations turns to shades of gray. Then the complexity of the drink better reflects the complexity of life and fits more neatly into the thought process. The man in his late thirties might regard some of the most recent lagers as tasteless, having no personality, devoid of interest. What he really means is its complexity does not mirror the complexity of taste that his mind requires.

The man in his twenties, who is still drinking these simplified products is not meeting complex woody earthy sour bitter characters in his alcohol consumption and is therefore not having his palate educated for say the complexity of a whiskey.

If he tries whiskey in his late twenties or early thirties, he will find it too difficult and too challenging. If he's not driven by a social need to enjoy it, he's liable to switch to the easier stronger alcohol effect of white spirits or of course wines.

Because wine has been learnt alongside lagers, is lighter, easier to drink, so the wine characteristics have become more fashionable. This makes the entry into the wine category rather than distilled based products less challenging. More complex wines, richer red wines begin to meet the need that previously whiskey had delivered. While at the same time social pressures had made the drunken Need State less attractive in people past their early twenties, it was inevitable that the wine and white spirit notes would largely flourish. Inevitably therefore brandy and whiskey characters would become less popular.

Certain products have been able to buck this trend. Southern Comfort is an excellent example.

Here is an easy to drink, but complex taste which avoids the bitter, sour challenging and harsh notes of other amber spirits. So younger consumers can enjoy it. They achieve a similar effect by drinking Jack Daniels and Coke.

So there is present within the taste palate of someone in their twenties only a few of the characteristics in the taste palate of some one in their forties.

The need for a wine character based spirit delivery is very apparent and indeed fruit based spirits have boomed in their alcopops format. It is even easier to consume a spirit based drink that tastes like a soft drink, so the teens do. The demise of whiskey sales is less to do with cyclic movement, but more based on the development of a different taste palate amongst the young generation that is now in its thirties. Few of this age cohort have learnt to drink the sour bitter difficult alcohol flavour.

Before we look at Wellness in the next chapter, the Harvey's Bristol Cream case study might elucidate. Here a superb world quality drink was being encountered by children at weddings and formal family occasions, before they had even consumed it. All they really recalled was the smell.

Its very powerful pungent aroma redolent of rich fruit cake or Christmas pudding permeated the whole room, filled as it was with ancient aunts, and doddering old uncles. To the young mind that smell and the occasion became paired and synonymous.

When in their turn the chance came to drink Bristol Cream, their immediate response was that this was old fashioned, dated and had nothing to do with them at all. Its competitor, Croft Original, a very light simple product in comparison, with substantial wine notes was the ideal alternative and it swept with extraordinary rapidity into brand leadership as the child age cohort mentioned above reached maturity.

In order to overcome this, Harvey's, working with the Marketing Clinic, optimised the Bristol Cream process, so as to lighten the nose freshen it a little and bring out the sophisticated complex but not heavy mid mouth tastes that highlight its sheer quality, verses its competitors.

But of course you can't announce you've optimised a product such as Harvey's Bristol Cream, so the message was communicated in another way. By utilising a completely different bottle, employing Bristol blue glass, Harvey's is of course from Bristol, you thus invite the next generation to take a new look at this product. Create a new "Encounter".

Perhaps it wasn't quite what they thought, and this bought precisely the element of newness to the overall experience that caused people to try it. It didn't announce the finessing of the taste because that would have massively irritated the heavy existing consumer group and would also have undercut all its brand provenance. Instead the visible newness content was restricted to this packaging element, but it was enough.

Those in their thirties immediately tried this new idea and lo and behold, the product hadn't got these ancient aunt messages, because the stimulation of the melody of taste and flavour had subtly altered and therefore the emotional message that was previously cued was broken. The product was evaluated as new.

The result, and a classic marketing award winning case study was that Harvey's Bristol cream returned to brand leadership. Its complexity of taste caused its competitor to simply seem unsophisticated, incomplete and less appropriate.

This is one of those rare occasions where because of the published case history we can tell the story and our role in it. But we have used the technique many times, and as long as the taste message and its emotional values are fully understood then it works.

Perhaps by now it is beginning to become clear that it is the emotional messages from the taste, be they of fashionability or Need State that makes the tastes themselves attractive or otherwise. The task is not easy. The search is for two, three of four flavours in certain parts of the mouth that trigger these redundant thoughts. Easier than a needle in a haystack, but not much! These few key flavours and the emotions they stir represent the "Taste Signature", critical to understand.

Next we look at the way in which attitudes to health have driven enormous changes in all areas of behaviour and most particularly in altering diet.

CHAPTER SIX

Wellness and Dietary Balance

The opening salvos were most probably the left and right of the learning that smoking caused cancer in '56 and the body bags returning from the Vietnam war in the '70s. Both of these appeared empirical evidence of unnecessary loss of life and the commencement of questioning about how to prolong life expectancy.

Heart transplants, heart disease and their connection with lack of exercise helped trigger the beginnings of the jogging phase. Here people felt that by taking this form of exercise they would improve their life chances. But there was a very important offshoot in that extended exercise releases stimulants into the brain which produce a mild high and feelings of euphoria and elation. This makes running addictive. At the time this was not medically known. All that runners were aware of was that they not only felt superb after the exercise but they seemed attracted to repeat the experience.

The next discovery was that heart disease is also affected by diet and not simply calorific intake but the individual ingredients themselves. Salt was the first criminal material. Excessive salt intake increases blood pressure which can precipitate heart disease and in certain societies, particularly the Scottish communities in America and Canada and obviously in Scotland, a tight connection was established. Salt became public enemy number one.

All over the Western world, people began to seriously limit the amount of salt used in cooking and very rapidly this spread to any criticism of consumer products that contain salt to enhance flavour.

Thus began the very first deprivation of stimulation through reduction in taste satisfaction at meal times, an issue that is still rolling today.

Next to come under the hammer was sugar, for its calorific intake and coffee began to be seen as an extremely dangerous stimulant. 'E' numbers followed and consumers for the first time ever read the packs! Shortly after this red meat was critiqued and the fat began to be removed from beef on the plate. Initially it survived in the cooking process. But not for long.

Now of course people started questioning all food and the thought process commenced from the other end. "You are what you eat" became a philosophy and so people looked for the positive foods that would do them good. Next fibre reared its ugly head and the dietary shift addressed the whole of the dairy produce area.

Dairy produce is full of fats inappropriate to adult consumption but excellent for growing children and thus milk then became semi-skimmed and finally skimmed.

With great skill therefore, the west has removed the two most important ingredients for carrying tastes through the mouth and therefore providing a feeling of satisfaction. Fat had been seriously reduced, especially saturated fats, and sugar and salt were now largely unacceptable, even at minimal levels. The food tasted awful.

Imagine the deep emotional satisfaction of eating muesli with skimmed milk, nicely balanced by some briefly frightened vegetables and just possibly some fish or poultry, with no stimulant to help you forget the meal!

Everyone tried this, but there was no emotional reward and people felt hungry all the time. Even such delights as fruit juice were criticised for their sugar content and so the vast majority of the public took cognisance of this but did not fully engage.

One can easily imagine what happened to confectionary. The other major culprit of taste and sugar delivery, the carbonated soft drink became the next target. Coca-Cola launched Diet Coke, a drink of a different footprint to the "real thing" but many consumers took it to their hearts and stomachs.

While trial of these broad brush ideas was fairly extensive, most notably in the middle class, so inevitably the market began to differentiate and fragment as different peoples tolerances of and delights in various elements of the total package began its inevitable personalisation. The contrary nature of the human spirit began to be applied to this new knowledge, which generally was accepted as a truth.

There was belief that if you limited your diet and took exercise you had every chance of staying younger longer, looking better and at the end of the day extending your life span. By the end of the '80s, the average young woman's dress size had, in terms of UK dress sizes, gone down from 12 to 10.

The first European generation to be well fed from babyhood then started to grow through and arrive as fitter, stronger, taller, heavier, whereas in the United States, the beginnings of childhood obesity began.

****

The '90s

By now diversity was becoming more extreme. There were those who endeavoured to follow the regime pretty thoroughly and at the other extreme those who rejected it out of hand and took little exercise and over-indulged. So hard and merciless was the epitome of the correct eating and exercising regime that it became stressful inspite of the elation of exercise. At first it was a difficult to follow the philospohy with measured enthusiasm – you either had to be obsessively committed or reject it out of hand. It lacked flexibility and reasonableness, if you couldn't match the standard, you simply gave up.

There was massive social pressure in magazines, television programs and at a personal level from people to conform. The discussion of these issues became a social norm. Questions of diet and exercise were asked at dinner parties, at work, even horrifyingly in the playground. So in order to conform, people felt they had to do some thing and this encouraged the explosion of badging and the use of the visible interpretations of such a belief. Now the clothes started to reflect this lifestyle, trainers began to grow into acceptable footwear and casual clothes swept through society.

Women played a vital role in this change. Firstly it freed many of them from the regime of having to produce substantial formal meals for the rest of the family. The new foods did not easily fit into the habit of three meals a day. And as family break up occurred more, at least in the Anglo-Saxon countries, but not in the Latin ones, so grazing by all members of the family started to become the norm. This was assisted by the arrival of the microwave and the further simplifying of food preparation.

There was little point in being an excellent cook if you couldn't use the very ingredients that produced flavour, so cooking evaporated as a skill but people still, through taste deprivation, hungered strongly for flavour and satisfaction. The pudding was now dead!

Most of the ethnic foods come from countries where the quality of meat was pretty low and the quantity minimal. As a result, covering the poor taste of meat and maximising the flavour spread had led to the growth of high impact tastes that satisfied through their flavour rather than through their sustenance. The human is easily confused between a high strong taste hit and a full stomach.

Many of these ethnic foods use fat, but it is concealed. It's not visible and many of the spices provide a substitute for sweetness. The West went ethnic food mad. Here was the perfect item – you could eat it, get maximum mouth satisfaction and feel, initially be satisfied but then after a short wait you were hungry again; but there still was that measure of satisfaction. Also because the ingredients weren't obvious, no one knew what they were eating so they had permission to eat it. The items were not on their prohibited list.

In the same way that the poor countries had produced their own ethnic diets, so had the worlds wealthiest. The American ethnic food, commonly called fast food delivers big taste impact, demands no table manners and is hugely portable, or at least definitely transportable to the home. Just like the other ethnics it contains strong sweetness, high fat content, but the western consumer, since this food is close to their ordinary diet, is able to recognise this and is therefore tolerant of third world ethnics but intolerant of the American equivalent.

The drive for greater health but also with taste took the northern European and American peoples to the Mediterranean diet. This looked like the solution to everything. It ubiquitously used olive oil, white fish, fruit and vegetables and a little wine. Here at last was something that was satisfying, provided decent flavour, required no chewing, it filled and satisfied. It also emotionally rewarded in that it was definitely healthy.

Next people sought to retain some adult balance once the first obsessions had worn off and people had looked for a construct of consumption that was more healthy but also satisfied. This meant that they looked in the round at their total diet, allowed themselves some indulgencies, if they'd been "earned" by a period of purely healthy eating.

That period could just be a couple of days before an indulgence was allowed and as a result, the pudding for Tuesday's midday meal could be enjoyed on Friday evening or Saturday morning and might even be a hamburger from MacDonalds. The irony of all this was that it had taken all the northern Europeans and Americans 15 years to reach the point where the French already were.

The French, terribly conscious of ingredients and the search for balance in their food and their strict Gaellic logic for its application were already eating a carefully balanced diet – rich, rewarding and fairly healthy. The Italians were better but rather spoilt it by consuming the worlds greatest intake per capita in terms of coffee and being some of the heaviest smokers on the planet.

Most cultures develop one or two superb uses of their local ingredients. And these were picked up by the world and globalisation of food proceeded the strict market globalisation that we currently enjoy.

If people are worried about their health in a pro-active sense and extraordinary circumspect about anything consumed, it was inevitable that heavy critique would begin about pharmaceutical products. The consumer rapidly became aware that anything that could help restore health also had side effects somewhere or another. There was therefore a strong drive to stop taking pharmaceutical products at all. These should only be used in extremis and there were other and better ways of solving the problem.

From this emerged the concept of holistic medicine. While this had slowly stirred in the '80s, by the '90s this was booming rapidly and has since become on full charge. The orthodox medical profession has resisted with extraordinary inflexibility the investigation of these classic or historical medicines. Connected issues like acupuncture, aromatherapy and yoga were part of the spread of new ideas. But they don't really deliver and only make small numbers of people feel better, enhanced or related.

Wellness is utopian. It is a concept towards which the public moves, but at which they can never arrive. It is as esoteric as freedom, peace or contentment. The human spirit finds it very difficult to enjoy a steady state and requires constant stimulation and aggravation in order to stay interested, involved and motivated. People feel an inherent drive in the direction of these concepts and are prepared to make many sacrifices to move in that direction, but they know if they arrived they'd be bored numb.

The pleasure is in the journey and the rewards lie in an extended youth and greater longevity. Recently as life spans have rapidly increased, so the interesting concept of taking care of oneself has sky rocketed, further fuelled by the demographics which has the baby boomers now moving into late middle age.

The wonders of medical science, heavily publicised and arguably the fastest growing area of current human endeavour is making the belief that nearly all things are possible. The consumer is therefore prepared to invest in anything that might extend the enjoyment and duration of their life. And while no one item is thought to make utopia possible, a whole raft of individual initiatives may make the progress towards this promise attractive and it all remains driven by the self actualisation which is at the heart of human ambition.

****

From the '90s to the Current Time

What is unusual about the learning process in this area of behaviour is that each new generation doesn't appear to reject the learnings of the previous one on issues of wellness. They simply respond to the stimulation of medical breakthroughs and the awareness of the growing importance of health. Unusually therefore each learning is grafted on top of the previous generations comprehension, and the movement becomes more extreme, more demanding and takes concepts the previous decade thought adventurous as the basic norm.

This has meant that today's younger consumer has eaten and drunk all the products available and fully aware of their image in health terms learnt to evaluate taste on a health criterion as well as one of pleasure and delight. This has also had the effect of marginalizing major themes and making them a part of the collective rather than motivating of themselves. This is the inevitable maturing of a market view.

At the same time the drug culture has impacted quite seriously on young people's perception of how food and drink works. The learning that a certain coloured pill produces a certain state of mind extends on to the belief that different alcohol drinks produce a different mood of inebriation. That's an important building block because it makes functional foods a totally credible idea. So today's younger late teen consumer sees nearly all foods and drinks in a categorising sense – they are good or bad, they produce this or that response from the body and give you various emotional rewards.

But they have moved on quite significantly from this point in that they now feel able to judge and categorise a food by a combination of its taste and the way it feels within the stomach. Many younger people, and girls are especially guilty of this, will reject foods that feel heavy or in any way bloating in the stomach. They are training themselves to feel mildly hungry all of the time. While the press blames the very emaciated world super models for enforcing this culture, in reality it's much more complex than that and is as much driven from the inner feelings of consumption as it is from body image value structure.

The consumer is therefore reacting intellectually and emotionally to foods consumed and their quantity, and making conscious decisions based on how they feel while eating, so as to match a recognised ideal.

The attitude to exercise is very similar in that there is not the same obsession as in the '80s but it has become more one of the elements of the way in which you should feel physically and physiologically, and the exercise regime is amended to match that judgement.

We therefore have a society in which people are more conscious of how their body feels than probably at any time since the classic Greek period. In effect the regime of the athlete is now moving through society as a conscious concept and model for their own behaviour.

Those of middle age or people with poor family medical histories are becoming much enamoured by the whole genome project and the way in which genetic engineering is suggesting the future will develop. The problem is that there is a wide clear gap between the expectancy of arrival of these breakthroughs and the reality of when they will be practical and readily available. The increase in the number of possible operations and the ageing population has put, as we all are aware, massive pressure on the NHS, but it is also exacerbated by this belief that more and more is possible and the consumers are very hungry for that result and today.

The fact that the population bulge with the middle age cohort is now moving through society will have an extraordinarily powerful effect on demands for this type of treatment as it can directly affect their life span and quality of life. The public has realised that there is a direct connection between hygiene, food intake, exercise and quality of life and life span, and that you can do something about it.

This means in real terms that consumers, at least middle class consumers, are making an individual and idiosyncratic strategy to encompass as much of this totality towards better health as suits them as an individual and is practical in terms of their life.

Therefore one should see all of these issues – medical advance, food and exercise as menus from which people will chose the pattern that works for them. It is therefore ludicrous to regard Wellness as a promotable property.

Wellness is no more promotable than freedom or happiness or pure pleasure. The consumer is totally aware of the menu and chooses consciously and unconsciously from it and anything that reinforces it that seems credible and fits them will be taken on board. As a result, to express the idea of Wellness is completely useless, it will persuade no one, but each element will be judged by the individual as contributing or otherwise to the life they want.

****

The Future

Interestingly the globalisation concept is definitely impacting on today's teens and early twenties in the sense that from a Wellness perspective, the western countries young populations are moving closer together. Whereas their parents are still consuming national traditional diets which are evolving to incorporate globalised food and drink items, they still keep to the core of their basic structure.

However, the teens are not doing this. They are much less aware of national boundaries, attracted to global brands and becoming more like each other than they are like their older generations with their own national characteristics. For example, the teenagers in Italy are now drinking more lager than wine, and the same is becoming true in Spain. In France, the young generation is embracing convenience and fast foods in a manner that horrifies their parents and of course in that way of balance mentioned earlier in this paper, ironically fast food is just as much a part of Wellness as is pure water.

Within the healthy part of their living strategy, the teens are increasingly judging food by how it feels and judging their state by how the body responds. They are more cognisant of this change than any of the previous generations and this suggests that as they move into their 20s, and indeed many are there now, that those beliefs will continue, and that this will impact on the way in which they bring up and feed their children. We've already seen today some mothers currently growing babies on a diet which reflects their own philosophy (light yoghurt!) and is entirely inappropriate for a child, but the coming generation will do this and more so.

It is easy to see that as this drive continues, there will be resultant health problems which will cause people to return to items that offer sustenance. Wellness will then not be seen so much in terms of always feeling slightly hungry and being conscious of the body's fitness state but will move to a greater balance where people are more aware of sustenance. As this pendulum swings back, perhaps the powerful position of high impact ethnic foods will reduce and the possibilities of extracting taste from within food itself from the cooking process of food will begin to re-emerge.

CHAPTER SEVEN

Tastes, Their Fit with Culture

The research foundation for this book's learning is built upon work on tastes and brands with consumers inside Europe, North America, and Asia.

The rise of food globalisation has been fuelled by foods and flavours from the fields, forests and hillsides of the entire planet. All of us have tried and tasted nearly every fruit, vegetable and domestic protein edible to man. The Multi-nationals have tested most of the locally successful brands found in the market places of third world countries. The winners are here in your local store. Dressed perhaps in Western clothing.

We have seen how the consumer can evaluate their product pre-encounter from signals and clues. The packaging, advertising and point of discovery talk to them. They bring to bear consciously or unconsciously all of their previous product food and drink experience. How they actually react to the product once it is in front of them and how it fits or otherwise with their anticipation will have a marked effect upon their response.

That collective learning of their life to date provides the judgement and the criteria of evaluation. We shall now see how the culture and the age cohort into which you are born has an enormous effect on your reaction to an identical offering, were it to be made.

If we look at different cultures it is inevitable that different countries will use the indigenous food items as the basis of their diet. They are available and cheap. The experience of many tests and trials in kitchen and factory evolve the best local experience. In this way food is no different from the geographical specialisation of industry in the industrial revolution. Indeed until serious international trade provided real selection most foods would have been very localised indeed. This restricted basket of wares forces, as hindrance frequently does, creativity from the individuals in the society. They labour to utilise as best as possible what they have available. The olive and coconut epitomise such exploitation.

We see in this the construct of the local palate of consumption. For that time. Let's just examine a few critical examples of this.

While civilisation was getting organised the quality of water was dubious in all countries. The safest way then was to consume water processed into alcohol drinks. This effectively killed off the bugs. It provided a good measure of taste and refreshment and unquestionably the happy buzz to arrive with the product would not have damaged sales. Alcohol, much criticised by today's killjoys, very effectively bonds together small groups. Ideal for a village community. Perfect for the extended family relationships. Currently and coincidentally, or perhaps not, unfashionable today.

Where the vine could grow, essentially the Mediterranean coasts, wine became the core consumption. Further north, with honey mead and with barley beer emerged.

Whenever there were attempts to contemporise and control quality, then local rules would break out.

An elegant example of this is in Germany, which laid down strict laws pertaining to the ingredients and processes that constitute lager. It was called and still is the Rheinheistgobit. This not only guaranteed a level of purity and quality, it also helped the indigenous industry gain a good foot hold. It was protectionist. It sheltered the brewers from imports.

Unsurprisingly also in the east, rice based wines and spirits became the norm. When the people of Europe, or at least a proportion of them emigrated west, so they took with then the concept of the drinks they had learnt to like in their own countries. This provided both America, and for those who went south, voluntarily or otherwise, South Africa, Australia and New Zealand with their own spectrum of wines and beers. All of which were adulterated by local ingredients and forged by climate and way of life.

The growth of beers was much accelerated where you had heavy labour. Whether it's in the mines of South Africa. In the prairies of the States. In the farms in New Zealand. Or under the anvil of Australia's sun.

Where life is easier in the Mediterranean climes, farming tends to be small, localised and just enough for individual families. From these spring a plethora of localised wines. The climate worked in other ways as well. The further north you go the easier it is to take care of meat. There you find a greater ritual in the consumption of red meat, often roasted and largely unadorned. Where the economy makes it a luxury filling items like Yorkshire Pudding bulk out the meal.

Venture south and sauces were required to cover the taste as the meat went off. And where it was in less supply and the weather was even hotter, in the Indian sub-continent then local spices and preservatives were used. These do more. They both conceal poor meat and their intense flavours create the illusion of being full.

Salting protein in northern countries would extend the period of time that meat and fish would be safe to eat. Smoking does the same thing and these very strong individualistic tastes emerged in those places. Bacon at the two extremes of the earth, smoked and salted fish around the continental basins.

Fruit, vegetables and cereals all had enormous effect on the localised diet. One can see in the US how the enormous wheat and corn growing ability of the central plains have driven the production of animals fed on grain not on grass. Stock grown in this way put weight on quickly and provide huge steaks. But the flavour is poor and light in the heavier taste notes.

This flavour deprivation has driven both the first and the more recent generations of American sauces. They really are needed in order to bolster the poor taste of an otherwise excellent quantity and quality of food.

Local climate has a serious effect on the availability and health of different domestic animals and their role in the various countries. Religions, ever pragmatic, create statutes and rubrics of diet and ritualistic preparation to protect the health of their fans. We are all aware of the Vietnamese penchant for the dog. But then perhaps very little other meat was available to them.

This pressure is not abating. Modern religions have great hopes for organic foods, grown for a purity notion and possibly good flavour. GM foods developed both for yield and increasingly medicinal benefits, create real fervour. But it incites many into invasive behaviour.

The voracious supermarkets demand that all fruits are huge, colourful, perfect and available throughout the year. A pressure that has shifted the demand to eating with the eye instead of eating with the palate. This is an example of a pendulum poised to swing back remarkably quickly when again taste becomes the issue of evaluation.

Then there are the imports, countries like Belgium, Holland, UK, Spain and Portugal with various levels of empire sucked in interesting and enjoyable foods, spices and sugars from around the globe. Inevitably individuals from those locations found their various ways to the motherland. They bought with them their cultures. Always of course heavily expressed in foods, and their preparations constructed from local abundance. Because food is paired with emotional experience, so an easy way to reinforce the emotions of your culture is to trigger these by eating the food. The cooking and serving rituals reinforce these feelings even more. You feel at home again.

Before we look at specific dishes and globalisation, other influential ingredients, in the construct of diet and therefore in the learning of an adult palate, in a particular location is the styles of family structure and eating. Both powered by local conditions and religious beliefs. The food speaks for its society.

It is always amusing to note the American perception of the Brits as stand-offish and uptight and the reverse view from the UK of Americans as intrusive and loud. But if you came from a small crowded island, you would guard your space and privacy. If you had colonised a wonderful continent with massive space and few people then indeed you would inevitably greet anyone you saw. You would be delighted to hear their story. Let's look at family structure and to elucidate this case choose Madrid in Spain and the Amsterdam region of Holland. These have been selected to avoid indigenous concern here in the UK!

In Holland the children are given very substantial freedom. This is almost certainly because the parents want their own, and justify this emancipation or lack or concern with various social arguments. Possible results of this strategy is a high divorce rate, a multitude of broken families and snack food eating by all family members. Does this sound familiar? Food can be taken at any time from a collective fridge and freezer, microwaved to a deliciously delightful perfection. It is then wolfed down, or rather up, as many people today eat standing up. Then the individual is off to the next exciting engagement.

This looks like real freedom, lack of excessive strictness by the parents and a more "grown up" attitude to the adventures of life. In that environment difficult concepts like drugs are legalised, and there are very few constraints upon behaviour.

In food terms this supports a snacking society supported by Holland's world wide trade links, plus the excellent availability of foods and brands around the world. So the young Dutch will grow up with a globalised taste palate, eating brands from everywhere but with a bias towards their own excellent dairy industry. They have superb milk and cheese concepts plus excellent prepared and smoked meats. Indeed their international trading leaves them with one of the worlds finest chocolate milk drinks. Much of Protestant Europe shares the habits if not the food. One thought that Luther had questioned merely the sacraments. Now we find he has altered the diet.

In Spain, the children are seen as the most valuable property of the family. The family stays together, divorce is at a very low rate and in the past Catholic views produced larger families. Although they are still larger, there is a shrinkage towards a more Northern European family size. However, their meals are held within the family and their main consumption is an evening meal. It starts at ten o'clock at night. This is made up of a multitude of different courses, all cooked with an abundance of fish and meats, with spices in the onion/garlic area

Even small children, two and three year olds, join that meal and eat a toned down version of that diet. The child is encouraged to have an opinion. It knows it is valued. As a result the teenage revolution is much subdued and definitely delayed through to late teens.

In food terms, therefore the Spanish child is soon drinking watered wine. But has grown up drinking some of the finest water in the world, because of course the arterial water from a country build on granite is likely to be much refined, superbly purified and of wonderful quality.

Culture and supply differences produce a radically different dietary experience. The Dutch enjoy more rich heavy full tastes, the Spanish more subtle, delicate flavours, wide in spectrum, but tinged with onion and garlic. Two areas of much of our research have been confectionary (Mars) and soft drinks (Coca-Cola). Clearly it's inappropriate to share these findings except to note how in these two countries the encounters with products in these categories are made at quite different ages. Speculate and your instincts will be correct.

Inevitably appreciation of sweetness levels, light and heavy tastes varies by country. Countries with historically poor diets, even if today there is plenty, often developed sweet palates. In spite of world class marketing efforts the respective national market shows position between Coca Cola and Pepsi can remarkably often be predicted by the taste palates of a countries residents. People prefer to eat and drink flavours that have functions structures and thus emotional meanings.

Finally, a few last thoughts on the construction of diet. Consider the Mexican diet and the Scandinavian, and just imagine the childhood process of acquiring the palates in those countries. Extend your thoughts to areas of strong religious belief, such as the Islam and Hindu societies. It is impossible to imagine that the appreciation of taste will be the same throughout the world. Of course it is not.

But foods always perform against a specific requirement, or Need State. So how can Mothers comfort a child returning home from school in France, Spain, and Holland today and England in, say, the 60s? In France, bread containing chocolate provides a rich in mouth melt. This reduces heart rate and comforts and is served as the goûté, when a child returns from school.

In Holland, again cheese is used but creamier milk drinks, chocolate again for its comfort and other dairy produce with their rich melt through the mouth are the products of first choice.

Of course in Spain the time structure is different, children coming home will be comforted by their superb natural water, which relaxes and reinvigorates as the individual is rehydrated. So comfort takes on a completely different meaning. We see Spanish water in a whole new light.

In the UK in the 60s a child was greeted by a cup of tea. When that generation of children became adults, what do they drink in stress? What a surprise. A cup of tea. Light and sweet in taste, gentle and warm to provide comfort. Followed by a gentle reviving through the flavour and subtle delivery of its caffeine. Some parallels there with Spain but in a completely different climatic circumstance and drug assisted. The child's need is emotionally similar, but the climates, societies, food availability and palate development are all different. To meet the need the Mother has to use that which triggers the right emotions in her child.

We've seen earlier that while the majority of the learnt palate relates to a culture, there are tastes and textures that transcend culture and innately work with the human being. So in every part of the world the diet consists of a combination of the locally involved items, structures and recipes plus the historical importation where the society had global interests and the exportation to the country where it didn't.

As a result there are a number of world wide dishes. Globalisation of the palate would be the contemporary interpretation. But it is not yet true. Most of the major cultures have produced some excellent dishes and while many are not yet world wide, an important number are.

Let's start at home. The British have exported bacon and eggs. But the world also greatly enjoys chilli con carne, pizza, pasta in a multitude of formats, sweet and sour pork, steak and chips, hamburgers and Coca-Cola. If we look within these western much enjoyed items and their cousins, Thai, Indonesian and Vietnamese foods, we find certain specific characteristics.

These foods provide a contrast in textures. They have soft and hard components, sometimes a crisp and chewy element, occasionally firm and rich saucy ingredients. The drink excepted, all give work for the front of the mouth and also a contrast in texture in the rear of the mouth, on which to chew. This makes the journey through the mouth interesting, stimulating and rewarding. You do not lose interest. There is tune in the taste.

If you suffer an eating experience in which everything is of similar tone, the human being gets bored stunningly quickly. We suffer from stimulation deprivation, get irritated and want to escape. We are a difficult species.

So great dishes need therefore to be this combination of contrasts which also encompasses light and heavy as well as crisp, chewy, granular or smooth. Also they have taste contrasts.

They have sharp, biting, aggressive, intrusive tastes combined with rich creamy heavier slower tastes that relax you. They tend to use sweetness and fat to carry flavour, whether it be through caramelisation in the cooking or through actively adding ingredients that bring these benefits to the item.

This type of food completely transcends Need States and is so enjoyable that it is often force fitted into an existing Need State in the importing country and enjoyed in a circumstance for which it was never designed. Sometimes the Need State is imported as well, the ritual of consumption and environment for social interaction just as stimulating and different as the food. They act synergistically.

The food is inherently so good, so enjoyable, so stimulating and satisfying that it not simply triggers the taste buds but also fires the emotional messages which make the experience particularly rewarding.

In contemporary terms we have seen this with branded food items which start in one Need State and transform to another where they are made to fit by the consumer simply because the taste is so excellent. It may start out as Party food, full of life and excitement. But it's so delicious it's eaten alone in front of the TV. Sherry and Ice cream. Pringles crisps.

What is particularly interesting is that the youth of Europe, the States and Australasia are moving closer and closer in dietary terms.

So that in Italy more lager is consumed by teenagers than wine. The Spanish mix Coca-Cola in with their indigenous alcohol drinks. The hamburger has moved across Europe. Pasta items are extensively eaten by this age group and products such as coffee are treated with very much respect and handled carefully by the young Europeans. Coffee is regarded as more dangerous than many alcohol drinks. How perspectives change!

They watch the same films, they wear the same clothes, listen to the same music. Follow the same celebrities.

They are the first globalised taste palate generation. They share more in common with their age cohorts three thousand miles away than they do in dietary terms with their parents in their very own home!

This will provide a revolution and a huge opportunity for brands to develop and extend world wide. These brands will find alarmingly high and positive responses, should they get the recipe, the taste and texture the eating experience right.

This is a movement on the turn. Winning a global race to match the emerging world wide palate will give unprecedented rewards. Many of today's monster brands will not make it. They were created in a different age for a different palate and Need State. They deliver emotions that are all less and less relevant today. It's an exciting future. Or a risky one!

In the next chapter we will look at the journey the taste makes through the mouth, how and why it triggers different emotions and therefore how its appeal is constructed.

CHAPTER EIGHT

Evolution of Taste Palette Preference

Taste mimics its time. The supply of ingredients and the public perceptions of recipes unravels within its epoch. The fashions of emotions come and go. And with these changes so the preferences for food and drinks evolve. It is never tranquil.

As can be easily imagined, all the events of learning tastes and their meaning in childhood and adolescence, experimenting with developments of flavours and new ideas in the teens, the encounters of numerous new foods, brands and drinks means that every adult builds up a whole series of taste preferences. Some of these are the innate key flavours that most of the world enjoys.

But these are usually raw ingredients. Most vary in their taste by growing conditions and their processing by country and region. Their mix and selection develops to provide a local interpretation. Coffee, tea, chocolate have wide differences in flavour round the world. Chicken, beef and pork reflect feeding, climate and husbandry practices. The flavour of milk and particularly butter is determined by the crop of grass and flora the cows eat. It's not just the process and salting.

Once these become an ingredient in a recipe they have mutated far from the natural taste. So even the innate flavours are adulterated. A final area is particularly interesting and very relevant indeed to the marketer.

The recipe develops the flavours of its ingredients, and this taste is then learnt by those in a society. It becomes closely associated with the Need States in which it is used. People in a society usually share the same everyday experiences and the individual flavours then come to mean the same to consumers of that age cohort in that society.

People develop a taste palate. A whole host of flavours that are currently preferred. This, unlike many other learnings, does not cause a food to be evaluated by conditioned response but a pro-active consideration of what that individual finds appropriate. If throughout life as each new taste nuance is encountered and as the myriad of taste combinations are met, each with the baggage of introduction, the consumer rather like an old city with newness partially overlaying older buildings builds up a taste appreciation against which almost all taste combinations have meanings. They have met and hold an opinion on most eat and drink experiences. They know what tastes right for them.

Let us chose a highly recognisable taste and break it down to explain the principal. Strawberry. To the British palate a suitably ripe strawberry will mean summer, relaxation, treat and substantial freshness.

But it will also, depending on how they like to eat strawberries be associated with a measure of fructose sweetness from within the fruit. Or if sugar is added the taste changes to include sucrose sweetness which tends to lengthen and deepen the flavour but reduce the top notes. Richer softer less sharp taste but easier.

For many its association will be with cream or ice cream. For individuals the spread of this encounter could cause the taste to range from strawberry picking with the family, and the resultant heavy indulgence in the taste for a short seasonal period, through strawberry as a component in summer eating to the rarefied atmosphere of and association with Wimbledon style occasions.

Different generations will also have different perceptions. Older people will be used to a smaller strawberry with slightly greater pureness but astringency of taste, often buffered by the use of the dairy fats. Use of cream were not frowned upon during their learning years.

The more contemporary the encounter, the more strawberries are likely to be eaten on their own au naturelle. But a child today might easily first meet as their encounter a strawberry in winter that grew in Spain. A very different experience.

But things have altered. As supermarkets have come to use fruits and vegetables as symptoms of their fresh foods philosophy so their in-store displays become increasingly important. Thus the appearance of a strawberry starts to take precedence over its taste.

Strawberries selected from warmer climes in winter are a harder more wooden tough eat. They have a dark red colour, they do have flavour but it seriously lacks the fresh top notes of a UK berry.

Strawberry as a fruit is available today with flavours from a green clean character with the strawberry purity following through into the mouth as the acidity hits. Through to a quite woody, chewy heavy taste which is rear mouth localised but with very little front of mouth freshness. Strawberry is also used as an aroma with creamy type toiletries for skin and bath. These tend to reflect the green end.

Strawberry is introduced as a medicinal taste to all the children in the UK through the brand Calpol. It's also used as a masking flavour for other medicines as it has when combined with sugar a good through mouth taste which has freshness and also depth. That second half of the taste within the melt tends to make it calming as well as fresh. It's no surprise therefore that its viewed as ideal for children's medicines.

But this flavour derivative will thus carry another learnt message. That of parental caring, concern and love but also of being at home, being cocooned and being ill. A very mixed basket. Strawberry could be met as jam, in yoghurt, ice cream or milk shake.

It's easy to see therefore that one taste family can have rather different meanings for individuals. But certain of those meanings will be stronger and more persistent because of the way in which that particular taste is encountered by a specific age cohort.

We can see that few, perhaps only being ill, of the above emotional connections or circumstances of use are emotionally negative. Indeed many of the associations are positive, associated with summer, good times, weekends, relaxation and indulgence.

However it is certain that each succeeding generation will regard strawberry as less precious. It is a fruit that is very difficult to successfully freeze and still maintain its texture and flavour.

But organised availability has radically lengthened its 'season' and its character has widened from a brief epitome of the wonders of summer through to just another fruit.

Strawberry on a cheesecake to some one in their 50s, a keen cheesecake age, will be judged against the real fruit. If you could persuade a twenty year old girl to try strawberry cheesecake, it would just be another flavour.

Her most likely preoccupation would be about the heavy fatty feel of the body of the cheesecake, the sweetness of the base. She would have difficulty not feeling that she was over-indulging and would be particularly disciplined over the next few days in order to compensate for that. Would the experience be worth the necessary subsequent restraint? Perhaps to the 50 year old, but not to the girl in her twenties.

So your peer group, the age cohort in which you reside, is critical in building your perception of and the meanings around an individual taste. It is extraordinary how similar are the consumption habits in food and drink terms across an age group. In each society everywhere within a country, people are eating and drinking products in a similar way.

This means that in broad, and often in quite specific terms, that each generation meets the same structure of tastes at roughly the same ages. Encountered in the same environment of consumption and Need State of eating. So individual flavours tend to have the same associations and meanings.

Of course there are always exceptions, people who's introduction was botched or for whom the association are not good or indeed the product delivery was poor on that occasion. This person will tend to carry a negative baggage in their emotional response to a taste where the rest of a generation may only carry positive messages. They often feel very out of step over this. In group discussions they frequently apologise for this difference. Conformity is a powerful motivator.

****

In a normal food or taste item, if we look at the taste characters met within different parts of the mouth, the mouthfeel, aroma and aftertaste, we will find 120-160 tastes within a normal food or drink item. Tastes also have shape. They have greater impact in different parts of the mouth. A dominant melt, aftertaste, chewiness or front of mouth taste hit. This is of great use when optimising the experience. The opportunity for improvement may lie in one of these areas, as the shape is better matched to the needs of the customer and the occasion. A coffee without some bitterness in the aftertaste will not signal caffeine and thereby dull its ability to awaken. Many people deliberately make their tea differently in order to enjoy an alternative variety drink at various times of the day.

All of this learnt opinion, different for each generation and separated a little between men and women provides a taste palette, like an artists colour range, where all the key tastes have specific meanings and carry positive or negative messages from the encounter, reinforced in their subsequent use.

But thus it is not cast in stone. People do develop life styles and philosophies and these opinions directly affect the food and drink they think suitable. Belief does impact on response. The devised philosophical taste choice can easily be acquired and evolve to become the preferred flavour.

For someone who has a certain commitment to balance within their diet, we find a constant if informal audit being kept of what they are eating. This for instance enables them to reduce the effect of an indulgent fattening taste consumption by subsequently consuming lighter, cleaner less sweet less rich other foods, until they feel balance is restored.

Today many consumers are bringing to their food strategy value judgements about how much or how little or how frequently certain foods should be consumed. This rapidly leads to being critical of certain mouthfeels and tastes. Unsurprisingly therefore the consumer will chose from the menu of all available tastes, mouthfeels, textures and aftertastes items that reflect beliefs in what should be their consumption. These will be moments of high discipline compared and contrasted with other more indulgent events.

What we are seeing here is taste selection based on foods that support their emotional beliefs. They wish to feel as though they are being true to their values. As a result they select what they consume by a total collective emotional response built on these life time learnings. This largely determines what they eat and drink.

****

But nature has a way of controlling extreme behaviour. The human being requires continual sensory stimulation. We need a range of experiences and therefore emotional responses together with physiological reactions or we rapidly become sensorily deprived and bored.

This contributes to why working with extreme diets has always proved untenable. People just can't adhere to those near starvation diets to hopefully lengthen life. Life might be longer on starvation rations, but it would surely seem so!

If too much monotony is maintained the emotional pressure for stimulation builds up. And up. The person breaks out of the discipline and moves to an extreme typically over the top response. The individual may not be addicted in strict terms to any particular consumption, but without doubt we are all addicted to a range of stimulation.

It is therefore far easier to tolerate some deviation from the diet and occasionally allow others tastes or emotions to be enjoyed within the balance of the core discipline. Once this is acknowledged by the individual it becomes quite practical to operate the new dietary change which is reinforcing the current value structure and life style. This balancing of satisfaction and discipline is the only realistic way in which taste deprivation can be coped with and managed, if you are trying to alter your previous taste palette.

Unsurprisingly, because the human is a social species and hence gregarious by nature, these changing beliefs about food and drink tend to be shared by many of those in society financially in a position to execute the strategy. Today those in their teens through to mid-20s have a view of consumption which is completely different to their parents attitude towards food and drink.

****

The balance of tastes that have positive and negative meanings alters over time. A meal, brand or beverage is preferred by one generation because it contained what was for them positive emotional values.

But equally it could easily contain (almost always a different flavour note) elsewhere within its flavour profile negative taste message which cause it to be rejected by the next generation.

Other forms of expression tell us that each generation respects little of the values of its parental cohort. Clothes, the performing arts, literature, entertainment, most change radically. Flavours go the same way, or have to evolve or re-present themselves.

Unless the moving palate is fully understood, leading brands could find themselves unaccountably slipping out of fashion. They often do. First there is a loss of frequency off use, which inevitably leads to a reduction in heavy users.

As the heavy users reduce, so the very presence of the product appears less it loses critical mass and its relevance decays. The light users simply don't come back and they lapse. The heavy users become lighter and suddenly this wonderful brand consumed on so many occasions by so many people is in serious decline. And it happens quickly.

To endeavour to prop it up by more advertising promoting its historical values or price reduction simply accelerates its decline. You remind the new generation of why they are rejecting the product. So they do. If the emotional messages surrounding it, delivered by its taste or mouthfeel are negative, the harder you push, the faster you kill it off. The problems within that taste experience have got to be understood deleted and the psychological message updated.

This is typified in the case study about Harvey's Bristol Cream, which is discussed in Chapter Five.

Current UK teenagers might take recreational drugs. They certainly blast themselves with high alcohol content drinks. Many appear to smoke with very considerable enthusiasm, yet most do balance this. It has become fashionable to only eat until there is a certain level of weight of food within the stomach. If the weight goes beyond that, or indeed the perception of the weight goes beyond that, they will stop eating. Couch potatoes excepted.

Politicians who do not understand this philosophy of the palate and the consumers judgement, assume that removing slim models from advertising would change this! Incredible! Misguided! Typical, address the symptom not the cause.

****

We can take this UK palate development in mind. But realise that most big brands are multi-national. One can imagine the problems of developing brands with a common strategy across various societies in which the taste palate and the psychological messages associated with that are at different stages of evolution. So often they are. Society and religious structures make a big impact on that taste palate through emotions, Need States and beliefs.

There is today definitely emerging some globalisation of the palate amongst today's teens. That globalisation affects Europe, US and

Australasia, but less so Asia or Africa. Asia is more flavour and ingredient aware than the West, but is interestingly less comfortable with emotional response to stimuli.

The Multinationals are not powerless. They don't have to slavishly pursue the different countries palates. It is possible to influence the taste palate. Big corporations should see their brand portfolios not as meeting a series of disconnected needs, but more as a process of educating the palate and communicating the beliefs triggered by the different brands' tastes and mouthfeels. It's perfectly possible to market a child's product that will predispose the child to prefer certain flavours in their teens.

This can then be structured so that the taste characteristics owned by the companies brands have a linkage through a life time. The brands are then acting synergistically to educate the broader construction of the taste palate in the direction of their choice.

Thus the marketer who doesn't understand the delivery in eating and drinking terms of all their brands and how this fits or doesn't fit in with the taste palates its values and emotions is flying blind and without radar.

The palate is constantly moving. It's restless. People seek new experiences in taste as in life. People become more fussy as they improve their quality of life. The wealthy are the worst. Today's popular flavour combination can be an anachronism in ten short years time. Your brand dies with it.

PART TWO

Manipulating Flavour for Marketing Advantage

CHAPTER NINE

Flavour Detection and Recognition

Taste seems a fleeting, momentary ethereal experience. Briefer, more transitory than an aroma. Normally with an odour you can, if you so wish indulge in a second sniff.

We cannot photograph a flavour, draw it or more significantly really describe it well. Yet it tugs at our emotions. Ironically its slower than we think, takes time to evaluate, it's a series of sequential stimuli akin to the frames of a film.

Taste takes a trip through the mouth, sensed and evaluated stage by stage. Finally it bequeaths a memory, very important in its evaluation. The aftertaste.

Like any journey that's full of interest the best examples gift a rollercoaster of emotions, from reconnaissance to reminiscence.

We have to detect and understand in detail the role of the various different tastes and textures within different parts of the total tasting experience in order to consider what may be possible. The components of this expedition, need to be deconstructed for the whole to be understood.

Usually but not always, the first awareness of a new taste experience is its visual impact. As exemplars let's examine some generic product types – cakes, meals and pies, confectionary and beverages.

Humans are extremely good at diagnosing the likely eating experience from inspection of food. They have much practice. In the instance of manufactured food they will interpret from sight the specific ingredients, textures and their balance in apparent quantity, and hence evaluate the flavour impact between the different ingredients. Anticipate the joy of the whole recipe's taste, not just the separate flavours.

If the product is a cake, they will examine the number of layers, the fruit, the cream, the jam, guess the likely taste and texture, the contributions to flavour and texture of the different cake types, shades and fillings. They will be able to judge the likely weight within the mouth and susbstantivity simply by looking at the cake texture and the contribution of each of the layers to the complete eat itself.

These cues suggest what it might feel like in the mouth, how firm, how soft, how delicate, how it will melt and how chewy will it be. A cake enthusiast is good at this. At the same time colour is very important. Is it bright, is there colour contrast? Does it look fresh? They want to see a whole mixture of tastes and to toy with the idea of a full bite in their mind.

Therefore colour gives them very strong guidance about flavour. For example, darker cake means richer heavier, a greater sugar, dried fruit or syrup content. Whereas a lighter sponge, both in colour and in the texture suggested by the aeration means a fairly insubstantial component – a lighter less serious eat! Self evidently, the balance between filling will also give away much. The whipped density and depth of fillings will suggest lightness or richness. The colours contribute greatly. They draw the eye. They excite and they help the individual classify from where the lead taste is likely to be delivered.

Thus the red spectrum works extremely well. This suggests the sour sweetness of certain berries, the firm chew of cherry. As it shades to deep red and purple the flavours richen and suggest contentment. The natural colours have vanilla, coffee messages and as they darken the richness of chocolate, alcohol or nut is suggested.

Simultaneously a cake is examined for its Need State. Is it extrovert and celebratory? To be this it must be extremely attractive, over the top and very colourful. Or is it packed with quality ingredients – dense and rich and therefore very satisfying, extremely relaxing, stroking almost. A more inner directed enjoyment? Any unfamiliar ingredient brings forth both an inquiry and potential excitement.

With savoury food not snack items, judgement is concentrated around the balance of ingredients. Where meat is involved, and it usually is, suspicion of quality or otherwise surrounds the size of protein pieces. The meat needs today to look lean. They may want to detect which cut is its origination. Indeed in most instances from which animal is the meat?

The components that go with this are searched, be they pasta, pastry or vegetables, for balance and suitability and therefore the likely taste of a single mouthful. This will determine if this product's going to be chosen.

Quality is much examined and is proportional to the correctness of the colours fitting the ingredients that they perceive to be there plus the identification of the individual pieces. While people can judge cooked food, work done for the UK Meat and Livestock Commission demonstrated that their judgement of raw meat is poor and ill informed.

With items that have pastry that is cooked, the external shape of this is a great giveaway. It needs to show there is fullness and generosity within, or an element of individuality in a mass produced product. The consumer likes to see highs and lows, contours and valleys, both in colour, with varieties of shades of baking and toasting and in rising of the material during the process.

With confectionary the colours must lead directly to an anticipation of ingredients, especially when fruit is involved. With chocolate products, the consumer almost has x-ray ability to judge the chocolate's thickness.

This is done by roughness of shape and the radius of corners which gives a reliable indication of the chocolate depth. This directly pertains to quality, luxury and weight of eat. Of course an estimate of the likely product interior, or is it solid chocolate, immediately directs the consumer to the Need State and the emotional experience of the eat.

If the product is really substantial then it's going to be very fuel orientated, it will fill you up, producing energy or indeed act as a genuine substitute for food. But if they anticipate, through the visual, a lighter lively product, snappy and texturally intrusive then they expect something to provide stimulation and a break in the mind set. This is ideal for a short stimulating snack, which will not satiate or over deliver on richness.

With alcohol drinks of course, the colour is a very strong indicator of strength of taste. So too is carbonation and head where relevant. They know that drinking through the head smooths and cushions taste delivery, softens the drink, makes it less of a taste hit and tends to carry the rear mouth flavours through. This makes the product a slower consumption and more reflective.

Equally of course, there is a high correlation between depth of amber brown colours and the anticipation of weight and complexity of taste. That rule is a pretty reliable indicator for all drinks, except that with soft drinks colour assumes a direct suggestion of flavour. Shades of colour are critical in driving the consumer into different parts of the fruits spectrum.

So for example with orange, the degree of acidity or creaminess in the colour cues the anticipation of astringency or weight and with it degrees of refreshment are immediately grasped. Pulp within orange is a major discriminator for usage, it reduces refreshment but enhances satisfaction. But children as a species will nearly always reject drinks containing 'bits'.

Illuminatingly many people find it easier to describe the taste experience of the item prior to eating it, since this is their normal thought process of evaluation, than they do when describing the taste once they have enjoyed it! Should anybody doubt the importance of the detail of product appearance on packaging, or the care exercised when choosing the individual piece of cooked merchandise, they underestimate human ability. We easily and speedily anticipate the taste from visual clues. It's a form of gestalt, completion of a part finished puzzle.

Visual evaluation is rational, deductive and conscious. The customer considers it knowingly. As a generalisation, drinks should shine with a sheen and foods look moist and glossy.

****

Next is the smell. The aroma is a big surprise. The majority of people, except with very well recognised aroma items such as bacon, eggs and coffee, use aroma very little as a diagnostic, even in the unconscious. They place far more credence on their ability to judge from appearance. But food aroma does sometimes triggers appetite and learnt emotional memories. The smell helping recall occasions or places.

This in part is due to a track record of being abysmal olfactory guessers and never really working the taste out from the smell. Also frequently they can consume the product almost immediately, so for many, why bother? The other difficulty is that some of the more important elements within the taste delivery, such as sweetness, sourness and mouthfeel, are extremely difficult to judge from aroma, unless it's extreme.

So here again, experience teaches the individual that the human aroma skill set is low, as a result it is used far less. What tends to happen is that certain aromas are critical as to judgement. Here we are experts. People smelling citrus are well able to judge the degree of juice, flesh, zest or peel contained in the likely taste and will apportion quality very carefully in terms of the absolute fruit content itself.

With tea the top notes from the aroma are critical as to freshness judgement. The consumer knows that if the tea doesn't have these green, fresh, dried grassy notes then it could easily be heavy, flat and stewed.

Coffee likewise. Here, the coffee smell is so evocative that people know the taste won't match the aroma. They still want the warm heavy satisfying relaxing notes of coffee to be present. They know perfectly well the taste won't reflect this, but they do derive much emotional familiarity and reflection from the aroma, which continues to be effective throughout the course of the consumption. All smells do contribute to the appreciation of flavour and medics will say that salt, bitter, sour and sweet are tastes the rest of the flavours are smells.

With foods the nose is a better judge of the cooking process than it is of the ingredients themselves. We can smell it's ready. Today the guilt associated with frying food, which is the chef's best form of taste transportation immediately signals unhealthy, thick, sticky and is absolutely outside your contract with your own eating strategy.

But sauces with their aromatic character tend to successfully cue the complexity and depth of taste. This produces an involving intellectual and emotional satisfaction of quality and encourages eating the food slowly with full satisfaction. In addition is also the enjoyment of both the individual flavours within the sauce and centre plate as well as the complexity of the total taste.

We have seen in Chapter two, aroma is a very powerful producer of emotional response. Cooking smells always suggest the delight and enjoyment of the social or individual break that food or drink brings. Certain aromas suggest party, celebration, others the trencherman's heavy delight. Yet other meat aromas hint at major rich goodness contrasted or co-existing with concerns about the evils of excess.

These cooking aromas also bring to mind such delight as the seasons, indoors or outdoors, intimate food, general family contentment or such esoteric issues as the weekend, freedom, holidays, valued moments, from different parts of the world.

The aroma is a major component in helping the human place and position the food or drink. Where did I enjoy this before? They may know when these notes tend to be part of their intake and the aroma triggers the associated emotions of that consumption occasion. As a result, they are predisposed to be in that frame of mind or indeed already are before they sit down to eat or drink.

Of course the aroma also triggers salivation. Indeed appearance can do this too, and this heightens anticipation, signals hunger and need, or indeed thirst. This anticipation acts entirely as an elegant aperitif for the item to be consumed. The mouth waters. You can taste it already.

So aromas greatest contribution is often scene setting. They can transport the individual to a basket of inter-related moods, almost a pigeon hole of a mood set. People after a good sniff can often select from a list of the appropriate words to determine the mood created by the learnt message from that smell. They can categorise aromas into their own response to them, be it excitable, optimistic, or aggressive. They were also capable of denoting the tone of the situation, the formality of the situation – is casualness appropriate or is it relaxed, serious, indulgent?

They were also well able to feel whether this aroma is trustworthy, reliable, safe, or edgy difficult and uncertain. Self evidently these different emotional results fit or do not fit different eating or drinking occasions and situations. Where the aroma message is strange or unusual it tends to be viewed as contexturally difficult to place. This is the moment, but is it the time for this food?

If the visual information suggests one thing and the aroma something else then people will practise avoidance, even before they start to eat. They are anticipating trouble. The food is left.

The same applies to their own judgement on what they do and don't eat and the relevant quantities. So at this point through appearance and aroma, they can anticipate how much they want to eat or drink of the element and therefore whether the portion size is appropriate or simply wrong for the likely eating experience.

Too many chips for me today, or the more complex "This sauce is too rich for my taste". Manufacturers make a lot of mistakes in this area in setting up through visual and aroma clues and eating circumstance, an anticipation, which their product then fails to deliver. This is easily got wrong by too much fat, sweet content or preservative which add weight when unexpected. Often there are remnant tastes or aftertastes within the finish which suggests the foods ingredients are misrepresented by the product photograph.

Every time you worry the consumer, you increase your chances of them not finishing your product. They have anticipated much of the taste experience from positioning, advertising and product shot, you must not misguide. People expect exaggeration and slight over claim. Yet it must not be directionally misleading. If they expect a healthy snack the taste and mouthfeel should be healthy. The quantity no more or less than a snack.

****

The consuming process is an area for incredible, almost unbelievable levels of manufacture incomprehension. The number of times we have researched very powerful dominant leading brands to find they are not consumed in quite the way the manufacturers understand them to be is extraordinary.

Products were always eaten or drunk within a range of different methods, but there are themes often well distanced from the obvious. Usage evolves as Need States develop until its quite distanced from the original understanding. This can lead to, and frequently does, wrong pack sizes, wrong individual product sizes, incorrect levels of flavour, carbonation and even alcohol.

This faulty perception is usually built on by flavour line extensions. These deliver tastes, configurations or sizes that through their journey within the mouth and therefore the emotional response bear a decreasing relationship with the way in which the original flavour is consumed today. They are too far from the "Taste Signature".

This leaves a bewildered consumer. The advertising and positioning of the total brand will often reflect some thing fairly close to the mainstream of eating. Suddenly here's an extension in size, shape and flavour that only fits a completely different Need State. This happens most with the middle-age/middle-class marketing syndrome. Here people who are too old and from a different socio-economic area of the market from the consumer, project their own beliefs directly onto the product. They make singular mistakes.

To consciously recall a taste people usually need a mental picture of the product in their mind. Try this yourself. Think spaghetti carbonara and try to recall the taste without a mental image. Then try it with one.

The circumstance of eating is often tied to the taste also. The learned emotion of the flavour is the real spectre at the feast. These emotions applaud or censure key tastes within the eat. They make or break the occasion. The diner is not conscious of the connection. They lie buried in the corners of the mind.

It is the balance of these messages that determine the emotional response to consumption. It is that emotional response that determines preferences. We delight or decry the food, yet we remain uncertain as to why.

CHAPTER TEN

The Taste Journey

Let's start with that journey of taste through the mouth. Let's see which emotional responses are born in the various parts of the mouth.

The front of mouth is associated with stimulation, alertness and swift response. This applies equally to taste and texture. So if you wish to wake up the brain, make the person change the direction of their thoughts into an active, positive even proactive fashion, then we need initial bite crunchiness and good front of mouth taste hit. Combine this with cleanliness, sharpness, freshness and lightness, and we have initiated such a response that previous thoughts are blown away.

So the tone for the whole journey of eating or drinking this product is set in train by the very first impressions. This is an important area of diagnostics and can provide emotional responses ranging from neutral or easy right through to wow, this is really something. You hear them all.

Sweetness of course is the crucial front of mouth impact taste. Flavours that have inherent sweetness or are indeed being delivered by sweetness, or the sweetness element within a complex flavour will be detected first at the front of mouth. The aroma kicks in here too helping diagnose the flavour and tripping off the learnt associations that accompany the note(s).

Already the mind is sorting messages. Do I recognise this? Instant comparisons are made. If I do, is it a flavour of which I approve – in the situation I am now in? To taste blackcurrant when eating a spaghetti carbonara would cause rejection.

Chicken tikka during an ice-cream would be difficult. A year after an individual has switched to diet beverages they will find the original product too heavy, far too sweet and sickly. Clearly these flavours are now for that person out of context.

The taste of pork in a vegetarian quiche will create shock and horror. These rejections are not just matters of appropriateness, many are based on beliefs! This first taste starts a ripple effect of judgement as to the foods energy suitability its match with current bodily needs and likely quantity to be consumed. If the initial taste is too sweet, people today will often stop consuming immediately.

They may have a commitment to health and to a balanced diet. This taste suggests neither. So it is rejected forthwith. This flavour is not liked. Issues of learning, belief and fashion. They dominate preference.

As we move back through the mouth into the pit of the tongue and the sides of the tongue, areas where acidic tastes are picked up, then the messages and frame of mind and judgement start to change. This area has taste receptors with more varied performance in detection. Food and drink tend to move past this area of the mouth quite quickly and the taste may be brief, and is often difficult to detect. Almost subliminal. People do however often first recognise complexity in foods here. They adjudge sweetness to be there but may not recognise its flavour at all. This message can be delayed by use of temperature, fats and pH so that it is first detected further back in the mouth where the deeper emotions are cued.

However in the normal course of events, the food now starts to react with the chewing process the temperature of the mouth or the melting of the flavours through the enzymes in the saliva. The melt is a critical transition.

This melt, into a liquor whose speed, richness and viscosity determines which of the myriad of emotional responses and associations this taste is going to create. If those emotions are currently positive and reinforce the eaters value structure in terms of what they (in their perception) should be eating then the taste is liked.

It is amazing how people can, through their beliefs, completely alter their taste palate. The simplest example is removing sugar from coffee. Once successful the individual becomes bigoted about coffee with sugar. Now she is absolutely unable to tolerate it. Often their rejection mirrors the size of the challenge, that giving up sugar in this beverage, was for her. Frequently it's the person with the most vigorous objection to finding sugar today in their coffee who had the biggest mountain to climb when they first gave up.

This melt and these messages are a powerful element in preference. As the melt happens, so different tastes are picked up at different moments by the same taste receptors. The sequence and change of notes within these complex flavours have a profound effect on people's enjoyment. They will not consciously detect individual flavours, except for those very few notes that they are fully aware of, but they will respond in a powerfully emotional fashion to this development in the taste journey.

Cakes and confectionary elegantly do this. Rich sauces bring this experience to savoury foods, with pasta as a particularly good neutral carrier of complex and rich melts.

A lot of foods melt at mouth temperature and flow through the mid mouth. The rate of flow is also very important as indeed is the feeling of weight and sweetness within the tastes.

The slower the flow, the deeper the relaxation, the more profound the reverie the greater the escape. All distant the individual from the current thought process. This is why heavy alcohol drinks, puddings providing after dinner sweetness are all part of changing the mood. A good cognac or Baileys are classics. Cheese cakes, death by chocolate and Irish Coffee all beautifully deliver these powerful emotions.

Whereas our sharp front of mouth ideal in snacks, perfect for soft drinks and sugar confectionary, accelerate heart rate, this melt or dissolve can to varying degrees slow the heart. This reduces blood pressure, helps relaxation and enables the enjoyment of those tastes to be further enhanced. A virtuous circle

By now it's obvious that the balance, nature of tastes, sweetness, fat content and richness and syrupy nature of the dissolve will all have varying emotional impacts. Indeed they do.

Not only does the texture, richness and weight of this dissolve signal messages and set up emotional feelings, but the flavours themselves have connections with different occasions learnt throughout life. Thus the message is a complex one and needs deconstructing. How much is the texture, of the melt how much the flavour, do they work in synergy or sequentially?

As the impact of flavour and mouthfeel varies with different foods in different parts of the mouth, so in compulsory unison the emotions are tugged along for the ride. This attracts, involves and captivates us. The emotional journey is the true reward. It is why you like the taste.

As we've noted different tastes impact in different areas of the mouth. But flavour has the equivalent of the acoustic echo, Doppler shift or venturi – the apparent source of the taste message can readily be concealed. It may be moved or even masked. Lemon is detected in the pit of the tongue. Its close relative lime very rear of mouth. Ginger rear sides of tongue. Initially this restricts the possibilities. Or so it seems.

But the mouth can be misled. Dairy fats in the mix tend to move the apparent impact of a flavour towards the mouths rear. Sweetness accelerates a flavours early recognition, helping to signal the taste from the front of the tongue. This is why sweetness greatly improves response to foods. It provides an early clear taste message. Also sweetness is inherently popular.

Acidity carries notes to the tongues sides, but carbonation widens the area of manifestation as well as greatly improving impact.

Flavours each have specific taste buds to detect them. But the medium carrying that flavour and the degree of sweet, sour, bitter or acid present can cause the effect of the message to seem to come from elsewhere in the mouth. The flavour can thus be displaced.

Temperature also has a great deal to do with taste impact. Both extremes of cold or heat significantly reduce flavours, some more than others. If a product is at one of these temperature extremes then the richer tastes, that would normally be perceived towards the back of the tongue and at the sides of the mouth and to the rear of the mouth will be noticed far less. Here the front of mouth tastes being less reduced will stand out more. Sour and bitter flavours survive temperature extremes quite well, sweet based notes less so.

This reduction in flavour delivery is not matched by a reduction in taste impact. Here we define the taste as sweet, salty, bitter and sour or acidic.

When chilled the flavour is reduced but the taste elements remain present and this enhances the refreshment. With a lemonade the higher acid content that is delivered alongside the lemon creates more of a taste hit, salivation is accelerated and refreshment results.

Not only do the receptors respond to the acid but when cold, carbonation is released not in the glass but on the tongue. This acts to exaggerate the impact on the receptors. The result is a harsh hit, almost on the edge of pain and maximum salivation and top refreshment.

In reality all that has happened is the cold drink has tickled their refreshing flavour responses and not actually refreshed them any more at all. Water in an isotonic format does that the best.

A favourite food or drink, just like a much loved book, film or piece of music moves us. It can inspire and encourage, excite and uplift or relax, calm or even amuse us. It can mother us, warm us, make us feel safe. Humans love emotional journeys full of twists and turns. Our favourite foods deliver the sequential states of mind we crave. These emotions drive preference and desire.

CHAPTER ELEVEN

From Melt to Aftertaste

The shape of this part of the taste is also very critical. Is the dissolve short and fast or longer, slower and deeper? Does it suggest fuel, or food that will eventually revitalise. Or is it much more indulgent, inner directed and purely for the contentment of the user?

The weight of chew, the effort required to generate this dissolve also provides powerful messages. Give the human an initial bite that is substantial or where they have to crack through a surface and they imagine real food sustenance.

Provide them with a lot of taste and much power and again they will feel that this product will really fill them up, make them replete and deeply satisfied. The individual is being tricked by the sheer power of the taste, irrespective of the flavours themselves.

Indeed there is much evidence that humans stop eating when they have enjoyed enough taste. They do this without properly judging the sustenance, the calorie level or the satisfaction provided by what they have actually eaten. Indian and Chinese foods are elegant examples of this. Marmite too.

If we are to improve the reception from the consumer to a food then we need to know quite a lot. What emotions are being stirred? At what point in the mouth are these being driven? Is it by the mouthfeel or the flavours? Which individual flavours are most responsible for the emotional response? Is it the melt or the aftertaste? The texture perhaps?

In real terms the solution to improving the products consumer acceptance is to reduce the tastes that signal today's negatives and enhance the flavours that fit the messages that either the brand wants or the consumer needs or of course ideally both.

This has an effect which appears miraculous.

Suddenly the consumer, bored and tired, with one set of meanings will take on board these new flavours and the attractive emotions they stir and preference will be transformed. The neatest published example of this in which we've been involved, was the work on Lurpak versus Anchor.

Within Anchor's taste and mouthfeel were certain flavour characteristics which were fatty, rich, heavy and very succulent. But these caused strong feelings of guilt for consuming so much lovely butter. Yet concealed within Lurpak were different, fresher cleaner taste characteristics and significantly those heavy guilt messages were at a lower level.

Consumers therefore imagined that what they were eating was a butter that had less caloric impact. The flavours might have been more subtle and harder to detect. But this was the direction in which much of the publics collective palate was moving, with this dietary preoccupation are fresh foods, vegetables and fruit. So it seemed to fit the direction in which they were going. The taste was fashionable.

In advertising terms you cannot tell the consumer these thoughts directly. They are both incredible, intrusive, irritating and do not motivate. The whole operation works at an unconscious level and the message needs communicating at that level. Enable the consumer to pick up those messages for themselves. It has to be their "discovery".

In this particular case an award winning piece of marketing, BMP's TV commercial supported by promotions, signalled through colours, shapes, lighting and foods these very messages. It worked, Lurpak's share surged.

When subsequently it was possible to produce a spreadable Lurpak by finding edible oils that held to the "Taste Signature" by having minimal effect upon flavour, and hence keeping the taste characteristics of the butter, the brand went on to take huge shares from the whole margarine sector.

In ironic contrast is the way in which margarines containing some butter characteristics and positioned as butter brands but carefully not described as margarine had done so well. Clover with multiple butter clues within its name, packaging format and colours, was placed on the table by a generation of Mothers. Then women described it as 'butter' to their children.

Extraordinary though it may seem, many late teens and early twenties adults think Clover is butter. After all their mother said 'pass the butter' at the Clover encounter and thereafter. When they passed Clover as butter, that is what it became.

We noted when we were looking at world wide food successes that a combination of front of mouth taste and mid mouth melt provided a wide range of emotions. This is important not only in that it makes the consumption experience an interesting and stimulate emotional journey but it enables the consumer to step off at any moment.

If they want the taste to be stimulating, they can concentrate on that part of the flavour and put to the back of their minds the deeper heavier emotional tastes and of course visa versa.

Any product that manages to do this can transcend the Need State in which it was first launched. It can intrude into general use, populating a whole variety of eating and drinking occasions and becoming truly a big brand.

Once the marketer has decoded the emotional, physiological and psychological messages from the tastes she is powerfully placed. She can enhance its ability not only to be more happily received by an evolving taste palate but also make it suitable for a wider variety of Need State eating and drinking occasions. Light users finding the product effective in these different circumstances become heavy users.

****

Finally on our journey through the eating experience we come to the finish and aftertaste. It is both in that melt and in the aftertaste that the deep complexity of taste versus aroma becomes more and more apparent.

The aftertaste is critical to enjoyment and carries enormous messages of permission to eat, drink or otherwise. The aftertaste is the longest moment of the journey. It is less flexible than any other elements of taste. Irrespective of the speed with which the product is eaten or drunk, the aftertaste remains the same. Temperature can have some effect but it's pretty minimal. Carbonation can alter it but again but not by that much.

Any food item is at first sight pretty much stuck with the aftertaste that it produces. The other characteristic about aftertaste which is so important is that aftertaste can build up. Since the aftertaste will still be present, if it's persistent at all, more of it is overlaid and the taste progressively increases in the throat. Rich foods and high taste items, such as ethnics, are guilty of this.

Australian lagers are the opposite, clearing from the mouth quickly. So there is no taste build, which has the additional benefit of making the next draught almost as good as the first. So you can drink more for longer!

The biggest problem with aftertaste is that any chemical ingredients or substantial food processing invasions in a natural taste will show up here. Sweeteners are classic for their domination of aftertaste. However the aftertaste, if it is well manipulated, can be very positive.

The aftertaste of alcohol is its strongest message and is a great deterrent to the younger drinker. If the sour bitter notes which occur rear mouth, especially the latter, can be reduced as in the case with progressively lighter lagers, the drink becomes easier. It can be replaced as is the case with Bacardi Breezer, then this strong sour taste message is all but completely masked. Here the final taste is fruity, with an edge.

Precisely the same applies when you wish to conceal a taste that you don't want present. For example, with Ice Teas, the last thing you need is a stewed tea taste rattling around the throat after a drink that is meant to be natural, highly refreshing and easy. With the Brits of course, tea means home and comfort. Its taste cannot therefore be faithfully reproduced in an Ice Tea with any hope of UK success. You have to be more clever than that. Select only those taste notes from tea that mean fresh and refreshment and lose the others.

Aftertaste is also the area interestingly of the greatest conscious application of critique. The consumer is fully aware what they are thinking so there is very little unconscious thought. When aftertastes are seen to be unpleasant, chemical or medicinal the product is rejected. So it is easy to find the error. The consumer does. This has led many companies to make serious mistakes in their taste developments.

Since the consumer can already recognise this and articulate on the subject, of course they do. As a result, the manufacturer thinks the aftertaste is the problem whereas in fact this is often untrue.

It may well be one of the problems but often it isn't the biggest cause of rejection, merely the one the consumer articulates the most. So they fix the aftertaste problem and immediately create others in the mid mouth where all the emotions, which actually determine preference lie. An easy mistake to make.

But aftertaste has one delightful characteristic. It can make a product Moreish. This means that there are within the taste, once the product has left the mouth, certain characteristics which make people want to eat or drink more. And more. We will look at this in greater detail later, but for a swift insight the following applies.

The first of these is a residual hint of that part of the taste that is most liked. This can be almost a memory, quite elusive, almost at the edge of fantasy. This is the right level. Make the memory of the heart of the taste too strong in the aftertaste and you have satiation. It's a fine line to run.

The person feels as if they have already had enough, the taste is still there and as we saw earlier the consumer is always confused between strength of taste and quantity eaten. So if your aftertaste contains too strong a hint of the taste that the consumers like then the product becomes satiating. They won't eat any more. So the hint needs to be just above this unconscious subliminal level. You can easily find this in the unconscious by working with the consumer in an appropriate fashion, but it must not be an excessively conscious or too overt a message.

Another trick is to dry the mouth. When the mouth is slightly dried, especially by acid, it causes salivation. This triggers the response to eat and as long as the taste is positive, the response is let's eat more of what we have just enjoyed. You can see the opposite occurring when the aftertaste message is both conscious and unattractive, 'let's eat something else to get rid of this taste'.

We can thus visualise a taste journey, that started with appearance and aroma, went through front of mouth, the melt of mid mouth and on into aftertaste. The different balance of flavour power within these sequential stages of the taste journey will again affect the emotions and the physiological response. Together these determine the Need States and the eating occasions of the product.

The pattern of taste as the product makes this journey can be expressed on a graph as a "shape". Appearance is plotted at the left through to aftertaste on the right of the horizontal axis.

The vertical axis shows where the taste is powerful in flavour and influence. Where it stirs the emotions. In each product category there is a right shape for success. This shape of taste provides a map for the journey of taste, mouthfeel and hence emotion and the holy grail of…preference and Need State.

Food or drink can be consciously engineered elegantly in its shape of taste to fit the emotions of the chosen Need States. When this is done well, it feels just what the consumer needed. Because it will be.

Chapter Twelve

Moreishness and Drinkability

Depending upon the needs of the moment, this can be either a powerfully positive or negative attribute. More interestingly it varies quite considerably by the type or style of food or drink involved. The elements that make certain food categories moreish are not in any way the same characteristics that will make a soft drink moreish. Moreishness is therefore very food specific, but in excess of this it is also quite Need State orientated as well.

It might be defined as a state of response to the food that once swallowed encourages you or even drives you to wish to indulge in more of the same product. It is not when one particular food item causes the demand for an alternate item to provide an overall in-mouth balance. It is a state of motivation for more of the same.

Repetition of behaviour can even be an element. Bite, chew, melt and swallow can all deliver moreishness but of these only arguably the melt could be regarded as taste or mouthfeel in nature. The others enjoy the psychological benefits of habitual behaviour. The bite can encourage you to keep going because it is a very stimulating and thought triggering process. So in eating a bag of crisps the first crunch which is with the front of the teeth is very satisfying. It provides an alert mouth and hence mind and this is of itself moreish. There is no requirement for flavour delivery for the benefits to be enjoyed, the mere repetitive crunching and the return for more is of itself short life addictive.

Chewing has a similar effect. Whereas biting is liable to raise heart rate and increase alertness, so steady chewing will lower heart rate, blood pressure, relax the individual. Often as a result it does provide concentration benefits as it cuts out from the mind the intrusion of other irrelevancies.

The chewing process creates salivation so it continues to be effective, even if the taste has long gone and the resultant rewards of calmness are often addictive. Therefore if something is chewed in an extended way without changing taste delivery, it is still effective. Of course the classic of this is chewing gum.

The melt is also a powerful trigger of emotional response and contributes greatly to the creation of an emotional relaxation whereas chewing will only maintain it.

Frequently the melt is such a powerful in mouth experience that you can observe people's eyes moving out of focus as their thoughts become inner-directed during that movement. It is when fuelled by the appropriate flavours and mouthfeels a very difficult behavioural experience to stop. It appears on the surface that many of the rich sweet products deliver their emotional peace through richness and sugariness but in fact savouries are just as capable of delivering the same emotional responses through their melt. Cheeses are an excellent example.

So the user enjoying this emotional escape delivered by the melt will be dragged from their reverie once the mouth is empty. The desire for a return to that emotional state, or better the steady maintenance of it encourages the eating of more of what's currently being consumed.

The swallow's interesting in that it is a reflex and not really subject to voluntary control. At the point of which the item has received the full impact of the in-mouth enzymes and is sufficiently chewed. It requires an act of will to avoid swallowing. As a result the swallow leaves the user bereft of the enjoyment and this precipitates as with the melt the desire to continue the process. This deprivation of taste stimuli rightly suggests that the main character within the taste needs to be lost following the swallow, or it will not be missed.

This is not the key importance of the swallow, it is that it commences the moment for arrival within the stomach. The stomach's reaction to foods that are substantial in their protein, fat or carbohydrate content, or indeed in their spiciness is to make a comparison with the taste hit to decide how much is being consumed. If the message is that not too much has happened, then full permission to keep filling the stomach continues.

Sweetness is particularly effective here in that sweetness alone tends not to produce satiation which is driven far more by fat based elements and therefore it's possible to go on and continue to consume even though there is much sweetness within the stomach. This reflex surfaces with small children who like sugar based confectionary and can easily eat it until they are sick.

The intensity of taste is particularly important here. Because as the intensity increases, so the feelings of having eaten enough start to weigh on the mind and the individual begins to feel full. As that begins to occur, so the moreish signals appear to switch down and the feelings of satiation begin. At that moment, that which has been driving moreishness goes into reverse and the consumer considers it time to stop.

They are too or uncomfortably more full that they personally belief is right for them. It is a very subjective view based entirely on learnt experience modified by individual value structure. 'I don't like to feel as full as this'.

If we use that physical eating process as a back cloth to understanding different food categories, we can now begin to examine the effect of the tastes and textures themselves.

****

Let us commence this evaluation with snack foods and let's address the savoury characters first. Snack foods are consumed in quite a wide range of Need States. They are much used as a way of providing a break in activity, and here the major criteria is front of mouth impact both texturally and in flavour terms. Ideally to go with that first crunch should be a substantial savoury taste hit. This awakens the mind, maximises the change of mood by causing current thoughts to be discarded.

This also makes the snack appropriate as a displacement activity, and we see its use socially in this fashion a great deal.

However if it is extended on it can deliver a measure of fuel and the promise of a decent return of energy. The taste hit at the front of the mouth promises all three and as the product moved from crunch to munch then its texture changes until it becomes a chewed mass out of which strong mid mouth flavours can emerge.

Snacks do not melt. At least savoury snacks don't.

They require the transition to rear mouth chew and the intense tastes usually built in that hit the front of tongue through a powerful combination of salty sweetness are very impactful. They used to have very little side of tongue effect and this is why acids worked so effectively in enhancing snack style products, hence the use of vinegar in traditional or in its more developed formats to go with the chips, savoury biscuits etc, which are snack orientated. Today the sides of tongue are more effectively addressed, but sourness must not be overdone.

Most savoury snacks are very short in their taste, very little occurring in the rear mouth because if too much is present there the taste will build. As that taste builds, so satiation begins and a product stops being consumed. Not really an ideal format for a snack product! The snack should be capable of being eaten until Doomsday.

You have to consume an enormous number of crisps to become full and usually before then the taste receptors receiving sweet and salty notes will be bombed out. It is this that will bring an end to the consumption. Here while there may be moreishness in the drying of the mouth, the strongest and most vital character has been the habitual repeat of the front of mouth crunching experience. But these elements do work synergistically, hence the huge success of crisps worldwide.

****

Sweet foods and confectionary are completely different in their appeal. Pure sugar based items carry certain tastes very well. Unsurprisingly a benevolent deity has made certain that fruit flavours are elegantly carried through by the use of sugars and therefore fruits work extremely well in these situations. However fruit means acidity and the pit of the tongue will receive the acid messages and these will build very rapidly indeed. Indeed the acidity appears to build towards satiation far more swiftly than the fruit flavours themselves or indeed the sweetness.

Here the enemy of moreishness is excess acidity and therefore sweet items based on sugar need to have low acidity if they require moreishness. The conundrum of course is that as the acidity is reduced so the taste appreciation of the fruit is neutered and a balance has to be struck. Even though the desire for more product may be created within the throat it is very nearly impossible to fill yourself with sugar based foods if the fruit characteristics are used. Essentially fruit awakens, enlivens and gives a measure of gentle stimulation but it's not at either extreme and contributes only a little to moreishness. So in order to become addictive sweet foods need ingredients that have long complex smooth melts. This means fats and ingredients that seem to melt in the mouth, of which more later.

****

This brings us to soft drinks which if they are fruit and acid based are stunningly refreshing, short in character but do not trigger any moreish response. The taste experience may be delightful. They may be wonderful on a hot day. They may be richly rewarding, but we tire of them. It's indicative that the least acidic and most gentle of the citrus fruits is the one that people can drink the most of.

Orange in its various formats is very kind, gentle, mildly acidic and does not dry the mouth to excess. This makes it possible to enjoy more of the product without satiation building up. At least in the UK the other major food flavour is the much developed and disorientated lemonade which has very few lemon characteristics. The minute you introduce the correct lemon characteristics and produce a quality product, you begin the process of killing off the possibility of its continual and excessive consumption. Grapefruit is never ever moreish.

If you wish to create a moreish soft drink then you need completely different characteristics. It is necessary to introduce richer taste elements that are quite heavy and substantial and indeed have a food orientation. These will provide a melt, which will of itself be moreish and if sufficiently rich and clearing of the mouth it will produce an excellent continual drink of which people do not tire. It can be sweet, dry the mouth, must be syrupy and rich if any level of moreishness is to be truly created. With sweet foods and confectionary the basis of moreishness is something quite different. This is in the area of deliciousness and almost always a profoundly rich melt, either a complexity of multiple different tastes, melting in sequence and extending the length of that melt, or a tighter richness with greater intensity.

Cakes would be an excellent example of the first one, count lines from confectionary have the same effect, but chocolate is a more intense taste and indeed too intense for young children, and so they quickly tire of the taste. Adults find the bitter sweetness with rich creaminess of chocolate, which has a lingering and sticky melt but uses bitterness to clear the palate, chronically moreish. Yet in dark chocolate the bitterness sweetness contrast is excessive, making it satiate its indulger quite swiftly.

****

Sauces are quite unusual in that they enable a food to change category. With the appropriate use of sauces, meats can be made into a pudding, difficult tastes can be smothered and the long rich flavours which provide the greatest degree of deliciousness can be created. And deliciousness is more effective as a moreish element than is any of the technical drying of the throat or the remnant of a hint of taste.

With care and subtle use of ingredients it is possible for the sauce to alter the Need State of the meal to which it is being added. In a casual eating society this can promote that meal further up the pleasure hierarchy and hence significantly increase its appeal and frequency of usage.

What the sauce does is stay out of the whole biting process but flows through the mouth with good front of mouth impact for lively sauces and a better, heavier rear mouth richness for more relaxing calming, peaceful reverie products. In nature, rich foods tend to be sweet. With a sauce without actually using any sugar based sweetness, it is possible through amino acids and herbs and spices to deliver a sweet effect which the mouth has difficulty differentiating from sucrose sweetness. As the sauce thickens and slows its movement through the journey of the mouth so the intensity of mid mouth melt is maximised.

The longer that process can be made to last the greater the perceived indulgence. Therefore, stickiness and the resistance to dissolving through the mouths enzymes will enhance richness and lead directly to the elusive deliciousness. However the problem is that as the richness is increased so the taste intensity will go up almost geometrically alongside. As this taste message builds to an over powering impact, the body begins to feel the onset of satiation.

The concern now revolves around 'is this too heavy? Am I eating too much? Today's consumer is very uncomfortable with this, and as the

European palate has changed and issues of wellness have become involved, so people are making careful judgements about what they eat. The moment this heavy message starts to be received, many consumers will start to feel guilty and switch off and stop eating. Therefore it is difficult to create deliciousness through sheer richness and it demands more melody of flavour to have the same effect.

Unsurprisingly therefore, as with most things, moreishness is on a continuum. Push too far the elements that provide moreishness and you immediately find yourself knocking at the door of satiation. It's a trick.

The need is to produce products that deliver complexity without too much density, richness without too much weight and deliciousness without too much sweetness or fat. The big selling world wide products that are effective at delivering this are mayonnaise and tomato ketchup and both of these have characteristics that avoid in the one instance too much taste satiation and in the other too much sweetness and richness impact. Yet they bring out the flavours of low fat less tasty items, or enhance those already fairly full of flavour.

It becomes immediately apparent that moreishness and drinkability have a relationship. Drinkability means that the product being consumed is highly sessionable and will not tire the user. In real terms this translates into demanding that the drink has balance within its character. If it has substantial taste impact in the early mouth then it's required to have some bitterness and sourness at the rear mouth in order to offset the front of mouth effect. This avoids satiation and leaves the consumer apparently just as thirsty as when they started.

Ideally therefore to be very drinkable, the mouth must not be radically altered in its taste state. If the mouth does go on a complex journey throughout the drink then it must be returned to a slightly bitter character which is interpreted as dryness. This dryness within the mouth therefore triggers the feelings of thirst, and encourages the movement on to the next consumption. So the product becomes highly drinkable.

The other way the same result can be achieved is through blandness. The drink having a sensible pH with flavours at a low level, all the elements not capable of being broken down entirely in the mouth and therefore travelling through almost without let or hindrance. Milk is an excellent example of this. The fatty deposit it leaves behind continues to make the consumer feel thirsty, and true experience shows that it's very difficult to satisfy thirst when drinking milk. It does not leave a clean mouth, or one slightly drying or even fresh and it unsurprisingly passes through and leaves behind deposits in a similar fashion to that of food.

Water is highly refreshing of course and it has the same effect, simply washing the mouth and neutralising it but not leaving any bitter drying or even acidic taste that would lead to moreishness. Again it's a very difficult drink to drink a lot of unless you are dehydrated in which case the body will send through strong messages. People who try to adhere to the two litres of water a day regime actually find it very difficult to do. It's unnatural and demands very conscious habitual determination to execute. Water's appeal could easily be improved with careful use of trace taste notes.

Drinkability is also reduced by temperature contrast. Drinks consumed at room temperature that are not too intrusive, where taste is not excessive and have a slight dryness are very effective, swiftly consumed and actually easier to drink large quantities of than water. The same is of course true but for different reasons for hot drinks where the heat dominates the taste message. Here a good example is tea. The drink cleans the mouth effectively and the aftertaste of tannin and the slight grassy and dried grass notes produce a drying effect. With coffee of course it's the bitterness which is also misinterpreted by the mouth as dryness.

****

In overall terms then, drinkabilty requires either a bland ease which tends to mean a natural ingredient which is not adulterated, modified, mixed, evolved or matured, an area where branding is always very difficult. The alternative is drinks that have moreishness which of itself leads to sessionability and heavy consumption. For a beverage to be truly drinkable it has to be sessionable and suitable to return to on a frequent basis.

One thought to keep in mind with sessionability is that the session is not just one occasion. A drink that has sessionability can be consumed at lunchtime with delight and three or four hours later the 'session' can continue on simply through a recall of that pleasure. The mind can hold the taste in the memory.

Those drinks that have high acid impact, much power and high refreshment satiate, and on the next occasion when the consumer wishes to return to it, satiation begins that little bit earlier.

As a result the individual tires of the drink and will tend to drink it a great deal when they first meet it, if they like it, but after a while the pattern of usage will stretch and the gaps between enjoyment will ever lengthen until the drink is finally dropped from the repertoire. Unsurprisingly quite small differences in foods and drinks exaggerate the consumers perception of difference if they occur in critical areas. Perhaps moreishness is of all responses the hardest to get right. But the commercial rewards justify the effort.

CHAPTER THIRTEEN

The "Taste Signature"

As we look deeper into the psychology created by the taste, we begin to learn many ways in which we can utilise this information. It gives us an insight into the brands relationship with the consumer, not otherwise grasped at all. It is at a different dimension. It communicates to the unconscious. It motivates and persuades. It is at the very heart of the loyalty of usage.

While you might wear the brand, indeed many do, as a way of expressing to others your value structure, you are wholly conscious of this but the enjoyment of the product itself transcends such values and works at a far more insidious and deeper level.

The shape of the taste encapsulates the impact upon the consumer of the different elements within that taste. They may be textural, such as mouthfeel, or they may be flavourful, such as citrus or oat. The important thing is that as the product is eaten or drunk and moves through the mouth, so different tastes, different flavours impact at different times in their journey and the emotions move with those changes to provide for those products one likes, a familiar and entirely positive experience. We have seen how those learnt values remain with the consumer for extensive periods of time, decades even, and it is them that guarantee the continued consumption and enjoyment. They only fade when a more appropriate or relevant series of emotions are driven by a new taste experience used in the same Need State.

The more contrast there is between textures and flavours, the more the emotions are moved and developed during the eating the more likely the product is to be popular and successful. Bland food and drink items tend to be more staples, providing bulk, background or length to other tastes. They may soften them, buffer them, make them last longer or ease them. But they are not the star. The hero of the eating experience is this powerfully emotive taste journey. So the shape really must be right and completely understood.

Should the food have a very strong front of mouth, either through its texture or taste, then it will awaken the consumer. This makes it appropriate for Need States where people want a break in their current thinking, to relieve them from boredom, or a way of holding their concentration during a repetitive task.

When the taste is more melodious and slow. Where it moves through the mouth with richness and weight, then the resultant reduction in heart rate produces a relaxed, comforting feeling. Many of the great commercial tastes have both characteristics within one experience, making it possible to utilise the product in a number of different ways. And thus it can be used on a host of different occasions where the emotional requirements are different and so the product is effective across a multitude of different Need States. This brings us to the famous characteristic of the melt.

The reason we coined this word was that the first time we discovered it was with chocolate. Here, a firm fat based solid melts within the mouth, both by temperature and enzyme action and goes from solid to rich syrup form in only a few moments. Hence the 'melt'.

But this effect, where the initial ingredients react to chewing, enzyme or temperature to alter the characteristics of the food or drink, can have the same effect. The drink can enrichen, thicken and coat the mouth. Many alcohol product do just exactly this. The sugars may emerge from within the structure of the food, as indeed might the proteins and fats. As this happens the taste seems to get deeper, more complex and profound. Then as it sequentially hits the taste buds through the rear of the mouth, so the complexity and richness causes consideration, reflection and in excellent examples reverie.

These are particularly rewarding experiences and because they are slow, they are much more noticeable and have a longer term effect. The consumer remembers them, delights in their return and is captivated by the flavour and emotional outtake. Unsurprisingly they return, seek the experience again and a loyalty towards the taste structure begins.

The Taste Signature is something rather different and particularly special.

Within the multitude of flavours and textures will be a precious few that are the most evocative of the delights of the particular food or drink. The smooth complexity of cognac. The rich slow warmth of Baileys. The wonderful crunch and powerfully persistent taste hit of Pringles. The explosive shattering at the heart of the Malteser. The wondrous bite at the beginning of the Mars Bar.

All of these are at the core of the taste signature of the particular product. But they are never as simple as described above. It is always a combination of a critical few four or five flavours, some textures, maybe a couple, and the movement or change in taste through the shape, possibly one element, that together makes up the taste signature. You could easily describe it as a footprint, because it represents the epitome of the personality of that consumption experience.

However of equal importance is that but epitomising the consumption it also crystallises the summary of the emotional deliveries that the product evokes.

When these are combined together we find a critical series of emotional responses generated by the taste signature itself. These two together with its critical few tastes and textures and the key emotional values they evoke are "The Taste Signature" of the brand.

This is very similar to finding the core benefit within a brand and is a piece of knowledge of equal stature.

For once you know and fully understand your taste signature, it can drive a raft of other marketing initiatives. Amongst these of course it can have a profound effect on advertising in terms of its strategy, because for the first time you possess the information for the real reason for consumption and can utilise this. But it is best done in an oblique fashion. Since these emotions are held at an unconscious level if the card is paid openly, the consumer will feel insulted and intruded upon and will reject the message. So it needs to be executed subtly and carefully.

Advertising is best used by exploiting the emotions of the experience, but leaving the taste message alone. We know the consumers are much more comfortable thinking in emotional terms, or at least they are in the Western world. Therefore the message is best carried out at that level where it will be credible, acceptable, understandable and persuasive.

It also can be used in terms of packaging, either picking up on the emotions, which can come through the packaging, or utilising appropriate colours or graphics to help communicate the taste without using the language. Taste is very effectively communicated by colour and also by shape, and this is a very good way of completing and fulfilling the message.

The real core benefit of understanding the taste signature is for the development of the brand. Once the taste signature is completely internalised by the marketers, it makes it possible for them to extend their brand. As long as they remain faithful to the key signature they can change the other elements within the brand and still remain true to the main cause of loyalty.

This means the consumer immediately recognises that taste as belonging to that brand, even though it is in a new format, or even a completely different Need State or other food category. This makes it possible to take a brand that is relatively small, or indeed dominant in a small category, and grow it elsewhere. Today with the costs of launching generating new brands being so high this is almost certainly the most effective way of moving a brand forward. Find the Taste signature – make sure you don't make mistakes.

In this way you take the signature, you know the priority of different elements of the signature and those that you might be able to bend a little and so extend the brand's reach and product formula. For example if you had a rich sugar and fat based melt as part of the brand, there would be nothing to stop you utilising a biscuit melt or even a cheese melt to produce the same effect. In this way the brand could move into radically different areas, but still carry the true message at the heart of the taste.

Understanding the signature is therefore the Holy Grail. This knowledge is of more value than any other aspect of understanding the taste delivery of your brand. It can even help you with cost reductions, or new processes and can make sure you remain true and faithful to the brand that the consumer knows and loves. It is so easy without this understanding to move outside it and make multiple errors. You see them everywhere. Brands extending ridiculously beyond their core competence simply because a few extra sales are generated. Eventually of course the brand is undercut and damaged and it's clear message is weakened.

The Taste Signature enables you to avoid all of these errors and at the same time take full advantage of the property you have. A taste signature is a corporate asset.

Here is a "Taste Signature" for an actual chocolate item (not a Mars product) to act as an example

Emotional Benefits Prioritised   *Taste Signature*

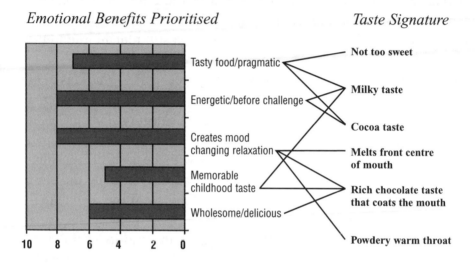

On the left are the emotions consumption create and their relative levels of importance. On the right the key elements of taste, flavour and mouthfeel are shown with the connecting lines showing how tastes trigger and drive these emotions.

"The Signature" can be also used for product bite size and shape, and particularly as a guide for line extensions. It may help other elements of the marketing mix and Need State targeting. Advertising Agencies often use it as input to the brand "Positioning".

CHAPTER FOURTEEN

Search Your Brand

One of the early signs that trouble is afoot with the consumption experience of your brand is that quantitative, ie numerical, taste research shows little variations when you make taste changes.

You keep receiving responses that show almost whatever variations you make the consumer perceives little difference. What this says is that you're changing the wrong things. The consumer in quantitative work will simply never give you guidance on what's required. But it does provide a very helpful and comforting sureness when your changes are better, if they are. But as a diagnostic tool it's of little usefulness. You are left not knowing why.

If this book has communicated anything, it is that tastes are preferred or otherwise and outside a narrow range of innately popular flavours, preference is driven by the emotional messages that different tastes, mouthfeels and aftertastes generate amongst your target market. When some of these become negative, more or less nothing else that you do will correct the problem. It may even accelerate the brands demise.

This is ironically why the 'cash cow' brands that have been milked and unsupported are actually, if you don't fix the fundamentals, behaving more sensibly than those who are desperately trying to solve the problem with completely the wrong marketing tools.

What you have to do is to start at the other end.

It is important to understand the environment of brands, beliefs and Need States into which your product arrived for the consumers. This requires that you understand the characteristics of your Need States in terms of precisely what the Need State requires.

How are they eating or drinking, with, before or after what? What is the social context? What in terms of taste, texture, mouthfeel, flavour characteristics, length of flavour, power of flavour, sweetness, fat content are right, and why do they work in that Need State. You will find that associated Need States have overlaps. If your brand is large, you will without doubt be in a number of such states. In some of which you will be more vulnerable to attack than in others.

For example, if you deliver a good bite, a solid taste, substantivity, rich full melt and a powerful aftertaste, you will do well when the consumer requires fuel. But if the same consumer requires an indulgent taste as a treat or reward, then the power and weight of your taste may by today's standards be excessive. Therefore you are vulnerable. If you expect to be eaten as a substitute for a light pudding such as a yoghurt, then your chances are very low.

Your brand is clearly a meal in itself and stunningly vulnerable in those other two Need States. We would expect a brand to be involved in four or five Need States, depending on how tightly we define the eating circumstances of those states.

At the same time you need to take consumers back to their encounter with the brand. You need to understand when their very first meeting with the brands was. How was it introduced, in what situation was it used, how did the product perform, how did it perform against they expectancy? Was it a taste that they immediately liked and which parts of the taste were initially attractive? Or, was it a taste that had some familiarity but the newness was difficult but intriguing? Did it therefore require acquisition? Many tastes that have become extremely popular needed to be acquired and learnt.

But that acquisition has to live in an environment of emotional values, circumstances and social or other interaction. Those psychological responses of the encounter will remain paired with that brand for life. So if your encounter is in a certain situation, is it altering or evolving is it different by age groups? Are younger age cohorts meeting the brand with different perceptions? Does it have a new meaning, what are those meanings?

Equally, since as we've seen that various age cohorts have their own taste palate, response is going to be different and the emotional reaction to taste is going to be practically disconnected. We have to understand how the recent adopters are responding emotionally to your offering and how they are categorising it. Because that is the way in which your brand has every chance of being restricted to in the future.

Once you have all these emotional values, you then need to understand your taste delivery versus the various user groups, Need

States, and your competitors. One of the big mistakes that one of the finest world wide companies I've ever worked with makes is that they don't look at their competitors. This makes it a constantly tightening effort around a single perception. Rather like driving a car fast through a telescope. Testing a short list of samples that vary on different criteria can be a reasonable substitute for evaluating competitors.

You need to see the environment in which you are playing, the contrasts and differences of your competitors and how they work in their and your strongest Need States. Starting from the users point of discovery and ending with their taste profile. You need peripheral vision and benchmarks to contexuralise your findings.

We need to understand the taste profile that your product has and what this delivers in emotional terms. Those terms are first established through learning all about the life long experience of your brand. Consumers behaviour, if they have known a product from childhood evolves as they are able to first select, then purchase and finally often leave the brand behind as a sign to themselves and their peer group that they are moving into adulthood. They will reintroduce it happily to their own children subsequently. But the second generation's value structure may be well distanced from the parental generation's point of view.

****

What you are critically after is finding which individual tastes, mouthfeels, textures etc are responsible for which emotional responses. You need to see how these emotional responses to the eat fit with the brand's range of emotions and also deconstruct the packaging and advertising and see how they perform against identical emotional choices.

Sometimes this produces an immediate realisation that all the elements of the marketing mix are not working synergistically. In which case the problem might simply be poor marketing. However, once you understand this tie up between the eat and taste experience evaluated against the emotional delivery, it becomes stunningly obvious why you are failing in certain Need States. You review why certain age groups are not as interested. Why you are losing out to certain competitors. Is it appropriateness to a Need State's requirement, or is it a product-brand issue of fit between these elements of the brands mix? All of this is the beginnings of knowing what to do about it.

In my experience, taste is like music. You don't need to remove a section of the orchestra (or range of taste), all you need to do is change the orchestration so that you hear the woodwinds more than before by making the strings more recessive. It's an issue of balance.

The consumer rarely develops their taste palate in such a way that tastes become absolutely unacceptable. What happens is that the balance of their acceptability, their degree of dominance or intrusion is too high or too low for the current palate. The taste therefore needs tuning to provide the right emotional message to make possible re-entry into the previous Need State. Or if the Need States themselves are evolving, and they often do, make certain that your product is appropriate to the requirements of the new and contemporary Need States.

We've been fortunate enough to work with a multitude of the world's leading consumer good companies. It is nearly always the case that they don't understand their brands in these terms. But equally it's frequently the case that small changes in product formulation can, when properly supported by the rest of their mix, have a profound effect in revitalising the brand.

Interestingly once the situation has been deconstructed and decoded and the problem slides into focus, it tends to be seen as obvious, and for everyone involved the learnings seem to fit in with at least one of their own hypotheses. As a result, redirection or correction is not politically or in real terms that difficult. Expressing the eat/drink in the shape of its taste format is often the easiest communication method. But clear comprehension of the "Taste Signature" is the best diagnostic.

But you do meet brands that cannot be altered. The corporate view is that this is our product and must not and cannot be changed. When that happens the task is much harder, but solutions can still be found.

Here, what has to be done is the characteristics which are most negative need burying and the positive ones require to be brought out. This has to be done so that the message is communicated at an unconscious level, with no description or explanations. The new message needs to replace an unconscious and unexpressed negative view. The new story has to be presented correctly. This means new packaging conceptually as much graphic as colour – but never by announcing 'new improved'.

Such overt copy puts down a conscious challenge and an unconscious belief which feels intrusive and contrary which leads to rejection. The consumer wants to find it somehow improved, not have such an 'improvement' thrust upon them. With such subtlety it is picked up without conscious thought. It is then believed and internalised.

Announce this change of emphasis in its taste delivery a part of the TV commercial and you've just shot yourself in the foot. The consumer must have this suggested to them, hinted through language, colour, other foods visuals and action and also role models, that those changes are afoot. This causes them to re-evaluate the product with the relaxed, positive mental attitude of an open mind.

Then their unconscious mind will pick up on those taste characteristics that you want them to, their emotional response will be triggered in the direction you require and the brand will seem revitalised. When this is done well the competition never knows what has hit them.

In an ideal world you often need to do both. Change the product, signal but not state that the product now eats or drinks more in line with today's market. Always let the consumer delight in the discovery, let them find how much better it now tastes.

CHAPTER FIFTEEN

Emotions from Flavour, Unlock the Opportunity

Once you know the emotions stirred by your product taste and you find which flavour characteristics trigger these emotions the rest is easy.

Once people are adult they only rarely meet completely new individual flavours. Frequently this is a component of travel and also the globalisation of foods being distributed widely. But in the main, most new experiences are remixes of previous tastes, as they may be constructed with original ingredients but built in a different fashion. The process may be different, or the source of sweetness, or even acidity might be new in that context. How does the consumer respond?

While they may commence their analysis of what they have eaten with an attempt to isolate particular flavours, spices are typically spotted, it becomes rapidly clear that they are not searching for the taste that they know, but more for the occasion, circumstance or place that they associate with that taste. The Encounter. Once they realise that they may have drunk this in a pub, then they work within that area of familiarity to try and find mentally the product that they feel is similar to the sample that they are tasting. What they are not doing is looking for the ingredient, much more looking for the emotional connection.

They will, with great articulation give a clear insight into the situation or place they associate with these particular tastes. They will provide also numerous emotional responses to the sort of flavour this is. They will associate a particular taste with particular feelings and this will come to the surface very swiftly.

What they will find extremely difficult is to describe the taste. Identify the odd flavour in the mix readily but describe it overall, no. This is at an extraordinarily high level of difficulty. Unless there are a lot of visual clues, they will be confused between a surprising array of alternatives. They may easily mistake strawberry for melon or cucumber, but what they will know is that this is a natural, summery or healthy flavour.

Sometimes a flavour and a texture are so closely aligned in their mind that the taste without the texture will be very hard to identify. The Germans for example have a very specific textural understanding of caramel and should this flavour be presented in a format that is not texturally correct, the people there will find it very difficult to identify. Unless the substance 'strings' when bitten and pulled it's not caramel to a German.

Of course what this means is that tastes and textures used out of the context in which they have been learnt can completely reposition themselves and provide a level of newness and familiarity which can fascinate.

****

Refreshment is interesting. This appears to be much more about a speed of reaction by the taste buds. An item being detected with great hit, presence and vitality will enliven the taste buds and produce a stimulation that is vibrant and has great vitality.

This could just as easily be a high taste food that you crunch as it might be a drink. There are specific ingredients that have these effects. Saltiness combined with sugar provides this level of stimulation. So does acidity which also delivers the archetypal refreshment which is astringency. Astringency is that rearward sides of tongue reaction when the mouth seems so dried that salivation follows immediately. The total feeling is one of stimulation followed by the watery effect of saliva.

Acidity tends to hit the pit of the tongue and this if powerful enough can add a very strong refreshing effect. This for instance is why sorbets are so excellent at cleansing the palate. High in acid, clear uncomplicated in note and with sweetness to carry them through the mouth and provide an astringent rear mouth reaction, they are almost ideal. Interestingly the consumers judge citrus fruits by their acid level as much as they do by their flavour. Therefore, as the acidity builds so they tend to revise their choice from orange through to grapefruit. However, excessive acidity satiates, and quickly.

Refreshment is also a function of liveliness in other formats. A front teeth crunchy snack product can even refresh. This is why lightly carbonated drinks are extremely refreshing. The carbonation dancing on the tongue, creating a very similar response, but twinkling across more taste buds than the astringency can do.

As the carbonation level is pushed up, so the taste is softened, smoothed, made easier. Drinks consumed through their heads, as are many beers, become kinder, easier, slower indeed less refreshing. If the drink ingredients are mid to rear mouth dominant, for example Whiskey, then the refreshment will be at a very low level and the emotional response will be redirected, and far deeper. These characteristics stir the soul.

****

Satiation itself is a surprisingly frequent occurrence, more so today as the consumer looks for more balance in their dietary intake. Currently this is quite a serious enemy for the brand. It is the opposite of stimulation deprivation. Here the taste stimulation is so strong initially and tends to remain in the aftertaste. Then the next mouthful builds it even further. This provides an almost geometric curve of taste building very rapidly until it becomes excessive.

It's a little bit like too much newness. After a point the differentiation is no longer possible and this one mix of tastes is so loud and the message goes into overload. Once that happens of course, the individual simply stops eating, or indeed they may switch to a drink to clear the palate, unaware of course that anything that had high refreshment or indeed astringency would ironically be effective. If the flavour is really extreme they may never even try the product again. Ever!

However if the taste that might normally provide the satiation is complex rather than inherently made up of one particular dominant flavour note then this will reduce the satiation effect. Instead the individual will begin to pick up as certain taste buds become neutralised by the first flavour and a different emotional message will emerge. This often produces feelings of sophistication, reflection and quality. Complexity softens excess.

Satiation also has the effect of confusing the individual as to the level of consumption. The taste buds are telling them they've eaten or drunk an enormous quantity and this will overpower the 'not yet full' judgement of the state of their stomach. We judge how much we need to eat largely by the sheer volume and quantity of taste that we've appreciated. This means that high taste items fill you more quickly and lower taste neutral items, especially ones of interesting texture don't have that effect. Popcorn is an excellent example of quantity being elusive to evaluate because of low taste and high texture.

Starch is used throughout the world to bulk up meals and also to provide a good balance between the stronger more satiating flavours from cooked meats and the necessity to take on board sufficient really satisfying food. Taste buffers assist consumption quantity.

As we found more about the different elements within consumption, it became clearer why all great dishes involve a combination of different strengths, styles of flavour, from the powerful to the bland and how texturally they are also full of contrast. It additionally helps if by judicious use of the eating implements you can alter the balance of taste between elements. This is something which one sees culturally, where the different ingredients are often actually served in different containers. This ability to mix also helps deal with the build up satiation and allows contrast through different balancing of ingredients to occur

****

Within the shape of the taste lies the keys to its usage, Need State and inherent popularity. The journey experience and the emotions engendered from sight of the food through to aftertaste and stomach has to be various, differentiating and thereby interesting.

Humans in their enjoyment of experiences need contrast and mix. All of the great and interesting people in history and personalities in literature and the performing arts are a puzzling mixture of contrasting characteristics. Some of these are positive, others are frequently very negative. It is this conundrum that fascinates us so much. Bad people are more interesting.

Therefore the eaten or drunk product needs to have these contrasts built within it. So that at some moments it might be sweet, at others sour, yet at other moments hard work or soft, crunchy and easy as well as having rich and light tastes mixed together.

The shape therefore needs to contain enough stimulation for the person's emotions to be involved and stirred and this is what makes it appealing. People want those emotional changes to maintain an interest and avoid any boredom. For the record, this is at the heart of the dietary problem of where people find healthy food incredibly dull. They tend to lack flavour, contrast and texture variation alone is not enough.

****

This contrast between satiation, the necessary emotional movement in the shape of the taste demonstrates readily how difficult it is to achieve the balance needed for something to be sessionable. Most people think of drinks in terms of their sessionability, and it is indeed easier to perceive in a drink than it is within a food, but the rules apply similarly.

Sessionability requires that the taste journey has variation but that it is not excessive. Too much taste, even if it's complex, will reduce the sessionability. The sheer weight of taste, even if made up entirely of much loved ingredients will tend eventually to become too much. So at the heart of sessionability is the need for minimum aftertaste. Or at least the aftertaste should be very fresh, clean, light and preferably elusive. What it must not do is progressively build up. It needs to diminish and rapidly.

It is no surprise that the hotter countries have made the greatest contribution to sessionability in beers. There, self evidently quantity needs to be consumed for re-hydration and so sessionability is a pre-requisite. The biggest enemy of sessionability is excessive sweetness, or indeed excessive acidity or sourness. But bitterness at a low level can be effective in maintaining the thirst. Careful balance again.

The interesting thing about taste levels is that if the levels are quite low, the mind seems to pursue the detection of the taste and so low taste can be quite interesting and mentally stimulating, like straining to hear a quiet sound, you listen more effectively. Yet at the same time light flavours will leave a clean fresh palate ready for more of the same. Saltiness of course appears to enhance taste, as indeed it does, but it also has the effect of increasing thirst. Judging how thirsty you are is difficult.

People will often think themselves thirsty when in fact what they are is hungry. Or to move on a step, what they are is lacking taste stimulation. Which is also why drinking two litres of water a day, unless a taste can be found within it, is a difficult habit to acquire and almost always is balanced out by contrasting tastes, taken at another time.

Outside alcohol drinks, sessionability requires softer, gentler, kinder tastes that have freshness and reasonable vitality to them. If they have become too complex, they begin to trigger comforting and reflecting thoughts which is a different form of session, constructed around emotional benefits. Of course, within alcohol drinks is the self indulgent comforting response the encourages reflection and quite free and unfettered thoughts. It's no surprise that this is used extensively to deliver comfort and escape.

****

As can readily be seen there is enormous interconnection between this short list of taste characteristics and they can be orchestrated together within a complete meal, ie through a sequence of courses, or be interplayed between food and drink to provide the right emotional context.

It is also easy to see why with food and drink stimulating so much emotion and thought that meal times are wonderful occasions for people to enjoy talk, exchange views and move closer together. The breaking of bread is a classic method to achieve solid adhesion. Better yet if there is more flavour.

When society moved to individual eating and snacking, it encourages distance between people and fights against the natural gregariousness with which people are most inherently comfortable. Food and drink are therefore very important in generating the values that are retained within the society.

In the same way we can track the contemporary issues by the changes in language used or appropriated for new meanings, so the construct of our taste palate tells us much about the society itself. Inevitably the two are linked and do reinforce each other.

Chapter Sixteen

Understand Your Taste
Improve Brand Performance

The work that the Marketing Clinic, the company through which this work is conducted, has done suggests that different companies find a host of advantageous ways to exploit this understanding of the messages within flavour. Marketers will be intrigued with some of the different ways the extensive blue chip client list has exploited this type of work.

There are a number of themes that do cluster and this suggests that these are the most advantageous for exploitation.

****

The first of these are Need States. By no means all leading consumer goods companies concentrate on the Need States of their product's consumption, but the best ones definitely do. The concept is to find the different circumstances in which the consumer eats or drinks their product. Clearly it depends how you delineate those definitions as to how many Need States you will find. However, in general terms it is best to re-draw the boundaries and leave yourself with five or six Need states for a product or product category.

If you develop more than these, firstly it will restrict your ability to retain and grasp within your mind the totality of the market. Secondly it's very difficult to market in a microcosmic way if the Need States become too small in their share of consumption.

Most brands begin their life with the consumer by being eaten in a very specific situation. This might means as a component within a specific meal, it may be as a stand alone item eaten for pleasure indulgence, comfort or to provide energy and fuel. It might even be a displacement activity with high tastes and crunch simply to give people something to do. A great way to beat boredom. We are all familiar with certain cocktail products which simply and only deliver that last function.

You need to understand exactly why the product works in its primary Need State. How is it eaten? Is it nibbled, crunched, chewed? Is it eaten alone or with other items? Is it eaten in sequence with other foods? How are other flavours and the journey of the taste through the mouth working in that Need State? What are the psychological and emotional needs of the state and how does this product, in detail, deliver those as an eat?

You also need to know what the product has replaced, what are its main competitors, and what within their eating experience makes them competitors and successes in that Need State? Often an evaluation of the key ingredients and their Need States provides great insights.

To do this of course you clearly have to have a complete understanding of the taste delivery, the physiological, psychological, practical and emotional benefits of your product versus a competitors and of course the total Need State.

It's useful to find out when the product was launched, what the consumers expected from its advertising, packaging and conceptual idea. And how this was delivered in reality once they started to consume. It is also imperative to understand whether this Need State is growing within society or is on the wane. If it's growing, from where, ie from what other Need States is it stealing. The reverse is required to be understood as well.

As consumers enjoy a product in one Need state, they will tend to utilise it in another Need State for which it probably wasn't created. In reality, nearly all highly successful brands emigrate from their initial Need State to populate a number of others or they simply wouldn't generate enough growth.

Because specific tastes or indeed quantities of product or mixes of flavours tend to restrict a product to a Need State, it's often wise to look at other tastes, packaging sizes and presentation formats in order to migrate the product into a second or third state.

If you completely understand your own product and the most adjacent Need States, it's not difficult to re-present it so that it can invade these other eating occasions and hence gain growth. It is also frequently advantageous to develop a competitive brand or add a line extension or reposition an existing other brand or sub brand so that between them they meet all the states that could possibly be covered.

A final thought on Need states is that constantly as life develops and changes, society moves on. The Need State sizes wax, wane and new ones are created. This is an area of major competitive opportunity. It is not difficult to change the total values in a marketplace by re-organising the Need States to fit an upcoming launch or reposition of your brand. If you are successful, the competitors will lose sales in a dramatic fashion. They will feel out of date to the consumer and of course therefore 'taste out of date' and become less attractive to consume.

****

Age cohorts can be quite interesting. As the eating and drinking habits of society develop, and currently the changes are more rapid than at any previous time in history, so the different age cohorts in your market will have different values. For the big brand this is remarkably irritating. They may be in a situation in which their consumer is loyal, eating across a number of Need States but naturally ageing. They are not recruiting sufficient new users in the upcoming age cohorts. And of course inevitably if they don't address this, the brand will diminish and die.

Interestingly, the younger age cohorts do influence their paternal generation. As they try new things, so their parents watch with interest and often will in their turn trial these new ideas. This has the effect creating a different style of discovery. The younger age introducing the product to the parental generation. A happy reverse of roles.

It is also likely with different generations that their requirements are radically different. It is without question true that the tastes that they have learnt to pair with different emotions and situations will be unlike those from previous generations. As a result they will inevitably when eating the product have an experience during which they will use dissimilar criteria of judgement, based on different learnt responses to flavour.

Since their taste and emotional balance are different, it is inevitable that within those criteria of judgement lie the difficulties of a brands consumption. Unless this is addressed in some way the new generation will not have the same educated response. They will never take the brand to heart. Its future is immediately restricted.

In our experience companies with big brands are always more scared of taking risks with their current heavy users than they are concerned about the longer term effects. Doubtless this is a function of the limited duration of responsibility that marketers have. Longer term solutions don't reward short term careers. So the youth end of the market tends to be completely ignored.

This is exacerbated even more by the 'middle age middle class marketing' disease where people tend to market to people they think are like themselves and not really grasp the views of other age cohorts. This is a rampant syndrome!

However it is also our experience that the loyal user is far more tolerant of changes within the brands eating or drinking experience than the company expects. Some may write to complain but very few change behaviour.

At the heart of every successful brand will be a very limited three or four tastes, a few mouthfeels, possibly merely a couple of supporting issues of appearance and particularly aftertaste that in reality constitute its appeal. This is the "Taste Signature". If these are seen in the context of the probable 120 tastes that are within the product, the three or four dozen mouthfeels plus the many characteristics of aftertaste it becomes apparent that if these core values are not damaged the product can be developed. It can easily be made more attractive without risk to the loyal user's continued consumption.

We have worked with many of the finest consumer goods companies in the world and have yet to meet one that completely understood the consumption taste and mouthfeel appeal of their big brands. Once that is completely understood then it's possible to develop the product so that it has greater appeal. That means the product itself is improved or the brand repositioned to provide more positive taste signals, to the younger age cohorts. Either or both of these moves lengthen the brands successful life.

For the record, retailers do understand this but not in taste terms. They continually flex, develop and evolve their offers but keep the core promise in the same area. This strategy here utilises the same plot that the retailers use but here it is applied in a sensory and emotional sense.

****

Light users are frustrating. Here is a bunch of individuals who dip in and out of the brand, use it with infrequency and seem not to engage with the concept of the consumption in any depth at all. If you examine the construct of their Need States, the answer may lie there. Many people simply never are in the situation or have the need that makes a product of value. In this rare occurrence, a product is perfectly valid and effective but the occasion for them simply doesn't occur.

Once that is deconstructed, the position is immediately obvious. However, often it does appear that the product could be used more often as they do eat competing items in the appropriate consuming situation. What is the problem?

If we lay to one side the issue of brand values and image, for this can restrict consumer use simply because the product has emotional values or projects an image that the individual simply does not wish to associate with. But once that is discounted our work has shown that in the vast majority of cases within that 140 tastes an mouthfeels of the product are signals that stimulate thoughts, feelings, emotions or physiological reactions about which the consumer is ill at ease.

This taste reminds them of emotions they don't like. That flavour is associated with bad experiences. This mouthfeel makes them feel fat. Those two characteristics in the aftertaste feel unnatural. The colour of the product puts them off. The texture is wrong for the flavours. Sometimes one of the characteristics in the aroma produces bad messages.

Essentially there are within the product tastes, flavours, aromas and mouthfeels they do not like, not because they are innately unpleasant but because the message they give is for them powerfully negative.

Of course if you chose an item that a nation is unfamiliar with then they will inherently find them unattractive. The salty liquorice taste enjoyed in the low countries and in parts of Scandinavia are abhorrent to the British palate. These are very difficult strong strident penetrating and pungent tastes and people just haven't been trained to enjoy them. It's no surprise that however often an adult Brit tries one they are never going to take these on board. A child might.

Also and equally important, should just a hint of that taste be present, then the total product will be rejected; because rather like the wrong note in music or your name mentioned at a cocktail party, you pick it up and it becomes impossible to ignore. The taste worries the depths of the mind.

The motto here is 'study the light user'.

****

The taste signature is a fascinating area for development. It represents huge opportunities and has only recently started to be exploited. And then frankly only by the very finest companies.

We mentioned above that at the core of the eating or drinking experience is a limited range of key tastes, mouthfeels, aromas and aftertastes that in essence make up the heart of the consumption appeal. They are likely to be effective in all the Need States. But it will be the peripheral flavours that help the product realign itself for consumption in different states and occasions.

This taste signature is very powerful and worth every bit a much as the brands perceived goodwill. Around this can be constructed a whole host of opportunities. The first of these is line extensions and brand developments into completely different categories. The consumer will never be able to express this to you but it can be found by sophisticated research methodology and makes it possible for a high familiarity and satisfaction to be guaranteed with this extension. At the same time there can be sufficient newness to revitalise, re-energise and push into either new users or Need States.

You see big brands who should know far better violating this signature. They allow their products to be served in a below par format with the signature damaged, broken or ignored. They allow packaging formats to break the delivery. They allow cost savings to chip away or new product processes to destroy their very signature.

Other companies have made a fortune and satisfied millions of consumers by taking that signature, almost always without conscious awareness that they are doing so, and building a raft of different brands. Each of these use the core signature and are therefore very likely to succeed. Both Unilever and especially Mars Confectionary do this really well.

We have begun to work on brand portfolio management with the more far seeing organisations. If the signature taste is fully understood, it soon becomes apparent that the consumer can be prepared to enjoy that taste when they meet it.

A good example of where this has not been done is with the amber spirits, particularly whiskey. Because the modern lagers have simple, light, uncomplicated tastes and lack the earthy acidic sour bitter and difficult characteristics of previous English bitter so the palate of today's late twenties has not been trained and prepared to drink whiskey. When they try it, the drink has so many foreign and difficult taste notes that it's just too unattractive. This causes the movement into other spirits, often white spirits, or into easier drinks or indeed into mixes or milder versions of the same product. This is partly the explanation for the massive success of Jack Daniels and Southern Comfort.

So a company could and should create brands for younger users that are trailing the tastes within their signature to lead users as they mature into their main big volume business. Bacardi Breezer is a good example with teenagers.

As we've seen throughout the book children's taste buds, their method of evaluating tastes, their desire for simple easy flavours that do not overwhelm their massive quantities of taste buds and have familiarity and repetitiveness are much appreciated. Children do not like dissonant tastes or complex textures, because the volume of reception is turned up so loud.

Also of course they are unable to classify each of the individual tastes into a like/ dislike or emotional meaning category. If a taste was not surrounded by any meaning of pleasure, enjoyment, refreshment etc then it's too difficult to handle and often rejected. As a result children's products tend to be very simple and are not required to deliver the sophisticated messages. Indeed they shouldn't be present.

What this means to the brand company however is that they need a child's version of their adult product. This should be a simplified version, easier to consume, softer, closer to the younger child's experience of the ease of mother's milk. The brand company therefore needs, in a perfect world, a small child version and a teen rebellion development.

The teenage transition is so important and the teenager requires to be perceived both by their colleagues and themselves as adventurous that teen products need to feel different. Here's a perfect opportunity to conceal underneath that heavy difference some powerful familiarity and educate the palate that this signature taste can also be a part of adventure just as much as it is safety, home and being cared for.

Some great brands carry these emotions within them and this enables users to spread from childhood right through teenage years into early twenties. Equally however there will be tastes introduced in teenage years which will be rejected when people move beyond that and other values become important. This is a core problem for instance with carbonated drinks.

This means that old established large brands need a younger version of the product slightly re-positioned and re-jigged for each generation to enable them to enjoy its discovery. But each time it should feed them into the core product in order that the major sales could be reinforced.

It is practically impossible to produce a single product that works from cradle to grave in terms of consumption. But you can find a signature that can stretch through that period. Many teenage products fail to transfer to adulthood because they do not offer the adult development. They are signalling too many of the wrong characteristics and therefore the product is dropped and not continued into adult life. Unless you completely understand that signature, and companies don't without massive help, then this development either within an individual brand or across a portfolio becomes frankly a lottery.

****

What area of considerable opportunity is also interestingly attractive? This is stealing your competitors signature. Marketing may be a commercially important and serious occupation but also it is fun. Looking within a major competitor and understanding its Need States and signature makes numerous opportunities immediately available. A few very large companies are both inflexible to change but also intellectually inflexible. They do not perceive the need to understand their own brand at this level in terms of their taste and psychological delivery and this leaves them beautifully vulnerable.

Their competitor can learn more about them than they know about themselves. It is then not difficult to take the consumers comfort and familiarity with their signature and the occasions in which that signature works and why it works and exploit that in new developments of their own. The iced lagers exploiting the characteristics of the white ciders is an interesting and elegant example of that. But here of course it was defensive, a reaction to lost sales rather than a straight opportunistic move against a big brand.

There are instances where it's done quite elegantly and at various levels. For example Lurpak's superb work on Spreadable, again a marketing award winner, managed to take the clothes and product benefits of the margarines and yet deliver a light elegant and healthy taste notes within butter. It's no surprise that this product was extraordinarily successful and ate heavily into the other brand's margarine sales.

Margarine has done it itself. Olivio takes the values of another category, inserts them into margarine and picks up the benefits.

Those instances of when it's done with competitive products and in a covert fashion cannot of course be discussed here, but they do exist and their invisibility is important to their continued survival.

As the cost of new brand launches becomes more and more prohibitive and the rewards less certain, one imagine that this theft of signature guarantees a measure of success, significantly reduces risk and will not be appreciated, understood or even grasped by the competitor becomes increasingly attractive. We expect to do much work in this area.

****

The last and major area where taste can be exploited is in its updating. Almost all successful brands owe that success to the appropriateness of the eat or drink to the time of their launch and during their subsequent life. However since each new generation learns a new taste palate with different emotional, psychological and physiological meanings. Attached to certain of those key tastes so inevitably the meaning triggered by consumption changes.

Each new generation is actually therefore tasting a different product in terms of their response to it and as this meaning evolves so it can move too easily in the wrong direction.

Yesterday's wholesomeness is today's too fattening. Yesterday's complexity is today's unnatural. Yesterday's comfort is today's overindulgence. The list goes on but it affects every single product in the marketplace.

These changes in perception and devaluing of individual taste characteristics is an undoubted component in a brands lifecycle. However subtle tuning of the product can have a remarkable effect. The brand can be completely rejuvenated without apparently what would appear to the consumer to be major changes.

The taste journey should be seen as a melody. If the woodwinds in the orchestra play a little more softly then the strings emerge more overtly. This is the game of tuning taste to fit current emotional values.

What has to be done is the Need States need to be completely understood to see what they are doing in terms of demand for delivery and movement within the using groups. This will give a clue as to the likely areas of problem and difficulty.

It is absolutely imperative that the individual tastes or mouthfeels responsible for those changes in values are detected. Also at the same time it is essential to understand that the core taste signature does not need alteration. It needs exploitation.

Then by careful development of the process, formula or recipe it is possible to enhance those positive tastes and therefore emotional messages and reduce or even eliminate the negative.

And with one bound the product is free. Amazingly the consumers evaluation of the product just alters and the messages become entirely positive. The result is a massive preference. A brand can in this revitalised form renew its growth.

It is remarkable how little usually requires to be changed. It is unsurprising because the core signature is most likely to be built around the longest term emotional values, those closest to the innate with the more transient emotive elements orbiting more around the edge of the taste experience.

All that has to be done is the changes made and the brand re-emerges, phoenix like, to a new phase of development, consumption and profit.

****

The final tuning once the major taste characteristics with their messages are fully understood is the process of tuning the taste. Coca-Cola Atlanta coined the phrase 'optimisation' for the process that we carry out. It's difficult to utilise quantitative research to diagnose the difference between the performance of different tastes and their emotional deliveries. Quantification of emotion is an elusive goal.

Quantification can be used to ascertain preference but tends not to diagnose the basis of that like or dislike. However, using our qualitative method that works with both taste and psychological profiles, we can soon find that the short falls tend to be provided by the delivery of negative messages which reduce the appeal. Once these have been bought more in balance by careful debriefing of R&D technical people. Then the message can be carefully re-engineered through the taste to match that which the consumer requires and indeed tunes in well with the positioning of the brand itself.

Once the food or drink is evaluated, it's then a case of describing in detail which part of the taste, mouthfeel, aroma or aftertaste are being successful and why and delineating those that require change or resolution.

When this has been found working with the consumer and the debrief executed with both marketing and R&D it usually follows that Research and development are well able to make the changes necessary to bring the product absolutely in line and optimise the taste and emotional message. Experience shows that when test samples are produced they should deliberately bracket the requirements by both under and over-shooting on some of the characteristics in order to judge degree and range of change.

This was always one of the larger problems when working with one of the best companies we have met on taste optimisation because it is necessary for R&D to have a clear idea of how large the change needs to be. This is best resolved by deliberately producing a range of variants and using those to provide scale.

Once the taste has been optimised then quantitative research provides confidence to go into various size of market test on the way to the products revision, re-launch or even a new products introduction to the marketplace.

****

All of the work encompassed in this book enjoys one very valuable advantage. Unless a company has worked directly with our system before then the work is new different and original.

This means that the political positions taken up by the various parties, the entrenched arguments throughout the history of the brand can be put on one side while this entirely new data and points of discussion are reviewed and digested. They change perspective and renew initiation.

This provides for all levels and disciplines within a company, a clean slate and the opportunity to build from scratch a new and deeper understanding. This makes the management of change an easier and less sticky challenge. As a result execution and movement to the marketplace tends to be much swifter than might be imagined.

The greatest delight and enjoyment is that the competitors never have the slightest concept of what's going on! Orthodox methods will not uncover the development and therefore it makes it very difficult for your competitor to commercially respond to these initiatives.

About the Author

It was while Head of New Products for Avon in Europe that Thornton Mustard first decided that methods for understanding fragrance preference needed to be developed. Answers from orthodox research were incomprehensible at best, downright misleading at worst. After being Marketing Director for Cussons and Managing Director for Wrigley's, both product areas very susceptible to aroma and taste perception, he set up the Marketing Clinic in 1984 in order to develop a methodology that could be applied for taste and aroma development.

The client list has been a marketing 'Who's Who':- Coca-Cola, Mars Confectionary, GlaxoSmithKline, Van den Burgh, Brooke Bond, British Bakeries, Mr Kipling, Danone, United Biscuits, Weetabix, Lurpak, Whitbread and Bass breweries, Allied Domecq, Bacardi, even Red Bull and Ribena. Projects have covered Europe, North America, Asia and Australia.

In an area where the technical language of flavour and food technology is separated by a chasm from that of the marketer and consumer, Thornton Mustard's work has provided a unique bridge between the emotions of the messages delivered to the consumer through the eating or drinking experience, which can be enhanced by product improvement.

When he first worked with Coca-Cola, he was told that the company had utilised their world-wide resources to find an alternative supplier in this area of work and was unable to find a true competitor.

The methods used to discover the true meanings of flavour have evolved, been developed and enhanced to the extent that product improvements can be incorporated into a brand which the consumer finds more acceptable but without fully realising that big changes have been made. They have also been greatly used on new and old product development. This story is different, original and we hope enjoyable. It tells how taste is about emotion and that it has a shape and at the heart of a brand is its "Taste Signature", a significant corporate asset.

Thornton Mustard lives with his wife and two sons on Dartmoor and in the Cayman Islands.